T0244103

CHRISTIANITY AND SCIENCE

Crossway Books by Herman Bavinck

Christianity and Science

Christian Worldview

CHRISTIANITY AND SCIENCE

Herman Bavinck

TRANSLATED AND EDITED BY

N. Gray Sutanto, James Eglinton, and Cory C. Brock

WHEATON, ILLINOIS

Christianity and Science

Published by Crossway
1300 Crescent Street
Wheaton, Illinois 60187

Originally published in Dutch as *Christelijke wetenschap* by Kok, Kampen, in 1904.

Cover design: Jordan Singer

First printing 2023

Printed in the United States of America

Hardcover ISBN: 978-1-4335-7920-2
ePub ISBN: 978-1-4335-7923-3
PDF ISBN: 978-1-4335-7921-9

Library of Congress Control Number: 2022056245

Crossway is a publishing ministry of Good News Publishers.

VP 32 31 30 29 28 27 26 25 24 23
15 14 13 12 11 10 9 8 7 6 5 4 3 2 1

Contents

Acknowledgments

Gray Sutanto: I am grateful to my wife, Indita, for allowing me many mornings over the summer of 2021 to translate this work while overlooking a beach in Bali. At that point, we were still awaiting good immigration news so that we might relocate to Washington DC. This book is a product of that wait. As ever, I am also thankful for James Eglinton's ongoing encouragement, help, and friendship. He is a reminder that one should always strive for improvement, not merely in the work of translation, but also in the task of theological scholarship itself. I am also grateful to continue to partner with Cory Brock, a wonderful collaborator and friend, on many projects. It was a delight to work with him on this as well.

James Eglinton: Once again, I am thankful to Gray and Cory for the invitation to join them in another Bavinck translation project, and for the opportunity this has provided to immerse myself in a richly rewarding text. Together, we are indebted to Justin Taylor and all at Crossway for their support of this work, for their own high standards in every regard, and above all, for their patience in awaiting the end result of our labors.

Cory Brock: It has been an increasing joy over the last number of years to work with James and Gray on numerous projects. We together share in the many benefits of learning from Herman Bavinck, and it is certainly so with this work. As always, we hope and pray that our work will be valuable to many. I am thankful to these two for our partnership and for James especially in his expertise in translation. It is a privilege I do not take for granted to get to do such work alongside my pastoral duties. I thus thank St Columba's Free Church, as well, for seeing value in scholarship for the people of God.

We are also grateful to Stephanie DiMaria for her thorough reading of this work, to Justin Taylor for his enthusiastic support of this project, to Thom Notaro for his careful editing, and to the entire Crossway team.

Editors' Introduction

To what extent, if any, is Christianity directed toward the life of the mind? In the early twenty-first century, many popular antireligious tropes paint conversion to Christianity as a kind of deactivation of the thinking faculties. Christianity, we often hear, is a blue pill that confirms believers to lives of thoughtlessness and stupefaction. And, of course, it is true that much of evangelicalism is marked by a profound skepticism toward all things academic. For complex reasons, evangelicalism has a deep tendency to separate the life of the mind from the life of the heart. More starkly still, evangelical culture often pits these against each other, mistakenly starving the head in an effort to nurture the heart. A quarter century ago, Mark Noll memorably summarized this particular context in the quip that "the scandal of the evangelical mind is that there is not much of an evangelical mind."[1]

1. Mark Noll, *The Scandal of the Evangelical Mind* (Grand Rapids, MI: Eerdmans, 1995), 3.

In the years since Noll's verdict, one point on the Protestant landscape—a branch of the Reformed tradition drawing inspiration from older Dutch neo-Calvinist sources—has been the scene of a notable renaissance in careful Christian thinking. At the forefront in that development stand the works of Herman Bavinck (1854–1921), formerly professor of dogmatics at the Free University of Amsterdam, and author of the magisterial four-volume *Reformed Dogmatics*—a text that is now available in multiple languages and widely regarded as a modern classic in the Christian literary canon. Bavinck's winsome combination of warm piety and intellectual depth has opened up a new vista for many current-day readers looking to move beyond the "heart versus head" impasse inherited from mainstream evangelical culture. In that context, in 2019, we published the first English translation of Bavinck's *Christian Worldview*; a short book originally published in 1904 as an argument for the importance of Christianity to the livability of life in the fractured modern age. Now, we have prepared the first English translation of its companion volume, *Christianity and Science*; a book written in the same year and intended as a kind of companion piece to *Christian Worldview*.

In *Christian Worldview*, Bavinck wrote that without Christianity, modern people are unable to hold together the essential shape of human life in the modern age: Christianity equips us with a view of life and the world that unites a sense of who we are, what the world is, and what we are to do with our lives. Christianity yields holism. In *Christianity and Science*, we find Bavinck focusing the same set of ideas on the life of the mind.

That human beings exist to love the Lord with the entirety of heart, soul, and *mind* is uncontroversial: it is the explicit teaching of Jesus himself. In much conservative Christianity today, though, the question of what this looks like in practice is much more fraught with danger, particularly for those engaged in the perilous world of ideas that is higher education. Is it possible to inhabit that world to the glory of God? Bavinck wrote *Christianity and Science* for those whose calling in life was to cultivate the life of the mind in precisely that setting: the university and college students and professors who, in the language of his day, were engaged in the world of science.

It is important for the reader to know that the English term *science* functions differently in its Dutch counterpart. In Anglophone culture, science is restrictively tied to forms of knowledge based on the empirical method and occupies a distinctly privileged position within the academy: to most in that context, a scientist speaks with far greater authority than, for example, a professor of literature. In our world, English speakers imagine the term *science* in a way that is profoundly shaped by the history of positivist philosophy (as will be seen in this book). The equivalent Dutch term, *wetenschap*,[2] is

2. Bavinck's original Dutch title, *Christelijke wetenschap*, is most accurately translated "Christian Science." However, we have provided an alternative rendering,

broader in scope and encompasses all higher forms of reflective, critical knowledge. As such, it refers to all that English speakers view as scholarship, while challenging the common Anglophone tendency to devalue the "nonscientific" sections of the academic community.[3] To Bavinck's Dutch ear, the question of whether a scientist or a theologian speaks with greater authority would make little sense: to him theology *is* a science, belongs in the university of the sciences, and is practiced by scientists.

If *Christian Worldview* was meant to be a sketch of the positive contributions of the notion of a Christian worldview as a whole in contrast to the modern worldview, *Christianity and Science* was meant to explore the more particular ways Christian faith can be generative for the academic disciplines. The book was composed of brief sections—here formatted as chapters—that concisely explore these areas. It begins by defining what is meant by the idea of Christian science—exploring both positive and negative examples of its emergence in the history of Christian thought—before moving into a critique of positivism. It then dives into the natural sciences, the humanities, theological science and religious studies,

"Christianity and Science," in order to avoid confusion with the heterodox Christian Science religion, which has no relation to Bavinck's work or theological commitments.

3. Bavinck was critical of the English language use of *science* on this point. See, for example, Herman Bavinck, *Philosophy of Revelation: A New Annotated Edition*, ed. Cory Brock and Nathaniel Gray Sutanto (Peabody, MA: Hendrickson, 2018), 71; James Eglinton, *Bavinck: A Critical Biography* (Grand Rapids, MI: Baker Academic, 2020), xix–xx.

the doctrine of revelation, and the benefits of Christianity for scholarship, before finally providing a sketch of what it means to develop a Christian university. In the original version, Bavinck covered all that in a brief 121 pages. Like *Christian Worldview*, *Christianity and Science* is a succinct text providing dense, but never turgid, reflection on an important subject.

Why do we think an English translation of this book is necessary? In his introduction, Bavinck himself offered four reasons that we believe continue to be resonant today. First, he argued that the impulse for the work went hand in hand with the construction of a new, modern, and explicitly Christian university: the Free University of Amsterdam, founded by his colleague Abraham Kuyper in 1880. Against those who claimed the modern age had killed any meaningful claim for Christianity as a religion at the cutting edge of human knowledge, Bavinck argued the opposite: modernity had set the stage for Christian scholarship to outshine its secularized rivals. The text is a kind of manifesto for this project that will continue to inform Christian educators in higher learning today—both Christian scholars in the mainstream academy and those who work in Christian higher education.

Second, Bavinck argued that Roman Catholicism had progressed much further in this area than its Reformed counterpart. "Logic and psychology, metaphysics and theology, history and literature, jurisprudence and sociology are practiced in such a way by them that the opponent must reckon with their work."[4] Ever since Pope Leo XIII's 1879 encyclical canonized a systematic philosophy for life based on the work of Thomas Aquinas, Roman Catholic higher learning had advanced with a united force that caused both admiration and trouble for Bavinck. In response, he argued that Protestants should learn from Catholicism's confidence and labors and provide a Reformed education that constitutes both a dialogue partner and an alternative to its Roman Catholic counterparts. A century on, it seems little has changed: Roman Catholic higher education (and in many contexts, Roman Catholic primary and secondary schooling) continues to operate with an intellectual rigor and intentionality that few Protestants can match.

Third, Bavinck believed that empiricism and logical positivism were losing their ground, and that immaterialist views of science were making a comeback in the modern age. He saw this in the growing influence of idealism and pantheism, which were winning the day over atheism and materialism as the prevailing worldviews within which the natural sciences were to be explained. In his view, this was an opportunity to showcase Christianity's insight on the "cause and essence of the things above," over these immaterialist alternatives.[5]

4. See p. 45, below. In this editors' introduction, quotations from Bavinck's *Christianity and Science* are cited from within this volume.
5. See p. 46, below.

Finally, then, Bavinck reasoned that the modern age manifests the undying human need for metaphysics and theology, as was also seen in the growing presence of "Buddhism and Islam" within Western culture in his day.[6] The previous century's faith in pure humanitarian progress had given way to a faith in a more cosmic power. Consistent with the current narratives that challenge the secularization hypothesis, history has vindicated Bavinck on this point. The world is not becoming less religious but more. A century on, while many secularized Westerners continue to ponder the place of religion in a scientific world, Bavinck's text challenges us to invert this perspective and learn, instead, to ponder the place of science in a religious world.

These four reasons—the challenge for Christianity to show its intellectual merits, the challenge set by Roman Catholicism's own example of tradition-specific scholarship, the demise of materialism, and the persistence of religious faith in a secularizing age—provided Bavinck with a clear impetus to argue for the benefit of Christian faith for higher education. A century later, Bavinck's cultural moment remains easily recognizable: Christians in the academy often hear that their faith is irrelevant to high-octane scholarship; Roman Catholicism continues to set an educational bar that Protestants struggle to clear; empiricism and positivism are a largely spent

6. See p. 47, below.

force, despite the presence of those who still cling to naive Dawkinsesque scientism; and both Islamic and Buddhist approaches to the life of the mind continue to make inroads in the West. For this reason, this text represents yet another first-generation neo-Calvinistic resource that continues to speak to Christians engaged in higher learning, and to those interested in exploring the benefits of Christian faith for all areas of life.

With the impetus for the work in view, we now turn to three observations that introduce the text: the *hope*, *definition*, and *necessity* of Christian science.

The Hope of Christian Science

Although many today would see the conditions of modernity as fundamentally unfavorable to a notion like Christian science, Bavinck's own vision of it was resolutely hopeful. He hinted at such in several remarks: "After the thirst for facts is initially quenched, hunger for the knowledge of the origin and goal, for the cause and essence of the things above, resurfaces."[7] In contrast to the antisupernaturalist drive that marked much nineteenth-century intellectual culture, he noted that the twentieth-century person was returning to the childlike longing for things unseen, for life behind the curtain. This was seen, he thought, not in a return to childish immaturity but in a longing for a proper sense of wonder. In that light,

7. See p. 46, below.

Bavinck cited one common way of marking the maturation of the modern person in the nineteenth century: "Just as, according to sociological law, a human being is a theologian in infancy and a metaphysician in youth, and then a physicist in adulthood, so humanity has passed through these three periods in science."[8] But now, having abandoned the transcendent and the metaphysical en route to the truly scientific, he or she changes tack, climbing back up the ladder to the things above. For Bavinck, this ascent is necessary because a person is driven toward facts by an investigatory instinct and, as such, is always compelled by the desire for unification by way of causation and value.

At the end of the nineteenth century, Bavinck thought, believers were jolted from their intellectual slumbers by the extent of the power of positivism and the fundamental challenge it posed to their supernaturalistic faith. Once again, believers had begun to take their place in that which was formerly neglected: the cultivation of the life of the Christian mind. Why? Supremely, Bavinck's "impression" was that "the banner of the gospel must also be displayed over the world of science."[9] What difference does the gospel make to the academic community? In both *Christian Worldview* and *Christianity and Science*, Bavinck portrays a human nature that is desperately thirsty for holism as a response to the sense of self fractured by empiricism. Again, there is a hunger after

8. See p. 71, below.
9. See p. 43, below.

knowledge of the origin and goal, after the essence of things. The childlike desire for unity of the self in a unified existence proves inescapable and even necessary.

If Immanuel Kant[10] had undermined the nineteenth-century mind's confidence in the existence and knowledge of God, immortality, and the soul, while replacing knowledge of these with an existential label of *necessary illusion*, then "modern culture" and its science, wielded by the likes of Ernest Renan[11] and Charles Darwin,[12] abolished even the need for that illusion in the hopes of progressivism—whatever that might mean for the modern individual. In *Christian Worldview*, Bavinck argues that while scientific materialism enjoyed a moment of dominance, the "youth of Zarathustra"—a new generation of atheists in the shadow of Friedrich Nietzsche[13]—failed. Contrary to that generation's expectations, religion failed to die, and the desired revaluation of older Christian values was seemingly ignored by most. And yet, the nineteenth century bred confusion: "Before all else," Bavinck notes, "what strikes us in the modern age is the internal discord that consumes the self."[14] The modern person was characterized by the denial (or perhaps more accurately still, the suppression) of the internal religious consciousness,

---

10. Immanuel Kant (1724–1804), a Prussian philosopher whose works animated the European Enlightenment.

11. Ernest Renan (1823–1892), a French materialist intellectual.

12. Charles Darwin (1809–1882), the English naturalist, geologist, and biologist.

13. Friedrich Nietzsche (1844–1900), the German atheist philosopher.

14. Herman Bavinck, *Christian Worldview* (Wheaton, IL: Crossway, 2019), 22.

which Bavinck sees as a sickness of soul producing a "disharmony between our thinking and feeling, between our willing and acting. . . . between science and life."[15]

Against that backdrop, "worldview" comes into focus as an inductive enterprise that describes the totality of the endeavor of the human consciousness to put philosophy and science within the boundaries of a map outlined by religion (with particular focus on epistemology and ethics). Alongside this, Bavinck's vision of Christian science focuses in particular on the relation between religion and the empirical sciences, between facts and metaphysics, and issues a call for their partnership.

The most obvious hope of Christian science, then, is the existential satisfaction brought about in the unity of metaphysics and observed facts. For "the metaphysical need lies too deep in human nature to be silenced in the long run."[16] In the early twentieth century, the resurgence of old and new religions was proof enough of this fact. Bavinck noted the growing number of his contemporaries, former scientific materialists, who had converted to spiritism, theosophy, Buddhism, and Islam. Reflecting on this, he wrote that "humanity is tired of doubt and uncertainty."[17] How should Christians respond in that setting? The return to positive Christianity had already demonstrated a return to dogmatics and church, history

15. Bavinck, *Christian Worldview*, 22.
16. See p. 47, below.
17. See p. 47, below.

and liturgy. In that setting, Christian science had also arisen, Bavinck argued, so that the mind and heart could live together in peace, so that a foundation of truth could be established, and so that places like the university—so deeply fragmented by modernity—could be whole once again. In the emergence of the Christian religion and its love for science, he suggested: "Christianity was the true philosophy, and Christians were the real philosophers. They knew reality in truth, they knew who God was, and now, equipped with this knowledge, they also had a different and better insight into the essence of the world, of nature and history."[18]

The Definition of Christian Science

In Bavinck's view, positivism was marked by a naive belief that empirical science is somehow neutral, objective, and presuppositionless—for which reason, positivists saw their approach to science as uniquely authoritative. It had somehow been freed from the bias and subjectivity that clings to our humanness. In response, Bavinck offered an alternative presentation of science, one that neither rejects the centrality of the empirical nor makes light of the metaphysical assumptions with which all humans proceed into scientific research. Bavinck made this case by arguing that Christianity enables the scientist to hold the empirical and the metaphysical together: ergo, *Christian* science.

---

18. See p. 52, below.

What does the adjective *Christian* mean for the scientific pursuit of knowledge? In *Christianity and Science*, Bavinck first invites his reader to consider the basics of science, in its essence and goal. Science begins with "normal empirical knowing."[19] The foundation upon which all science stands is the assumption of the unity of subject and object in normal empirical knowing (which, he argues, positivism fails to reckon with). Within normal knowing, there are degrees of certainty. While we may refer to many different propositions as objects of knowledge, we also know the implicit differences in knowing, believing, and assuming, all of which Bavinck sees as aspects of knowledge. For example, "believing stands beneath knowing [*weten*] not in subjective assurance but in objective obviousness."[20] Believing is so important, Bavinck argues, because most of what we know in life is not the product of objective obviousness. Rather, we receive much of our "knowledge" by way of trusted authority. When human beings arrive at a place where their daily needs are met, they desire to move beyond "normal empirical knowing" toward methodological knowing—a product of careful, controlled, systematic research and reflection on what is. This move from untested received knowledge toward a tested refinement of knowledge is the next move in the development of science. But again,

19. See p. 107, below.

20. See p. 109, below. The Dutch verbs *weten* and *kennen* deal, respectively, with more objective, reflective (*weten*) and subjective, personal (*kennen*) forms of knowledge.

humans are not satisfied with a systematic presentation of what is (only according to the senses). Such endeavors do require the uncovering of causes and natures, but a person also wants to know *why*. An exclusive diet of *what* answers leaves the stomach empty. While certain investigations might produce some immediate, obvious answers to the questions like *for what purpose?* empirical knowing remains ultimately inadequate in binding the truth to the realm of the ideal. It cannot posit final causes. It has no word to the ultimate, existential questions of *why*.

For this reason, Bavinck argues, science and philosophy are bound together as "physics" and "meta-physics." From such desire and necessity, institutions like the university arise. Bavinck explains this relation in this lengthy yet helpful quote:

> What now belongs under the rubric of scientific research and, as such, has a right to the name *science* is not decided by us a priori, but is rather provided in the passage of history [*historie*] and produced by its events [*geschiedenis*]. Slowly, investigation, the remit of science, the extent of the university, stretches out. Scientific thinking began in Greece with the question of the final ground of things, and from there, all the problems that present themselves to the human mind [*geest*] were developed in good order. The universities were not set up artificially in the Middle Ages,

> according to a previously established schema but, rather, were first planted as a small sprig, from which they grew like a living organism. In the present day, the technical subjects are gradually elevating themselves to the highest point of the university's sciences, and these are constantly subject to a powerful evolution. In one word, there has been a development of science in the events of history [*geschiedenis*] that does not happen outside of human thinking and willing, but that also cannot be explained from these, and that points back to a driving idea, to an organized thought.[21]

Thus, while there is a difference between "normal" and "scientific" knowing, the two exist in the same continuum: "Empirical knowing [*weten*] knows [*kent*] the particular, independent phenomena, but scientific knowing [*weten*] seeks the universal, the law, that masters them all, the idea that animates them all."[22] And if science seeks the universal, the idea, then it is quite possible to speak of "Christian science." What is Bavinck trying to accomplish by the use of this adjective? As he puts it, "The end goal of science can be none other than the knowledge of the truth—of the full, pure truth."[23]

If one has found the full, pure truth by faith, then it is impossible and even wrong, he supposes, for this ideal

21. See p. 113, below.
22. See p. 114, below.
23. See p. 127, below.

to be disallowed once that person steps into the arena of science. A Christian practitioner of science must not be expected to imagine he or she is some other sort of person simply by virtue of the scientific task. Indeed, an expectation that a believer will somehow ignore or deactivate his or her most basic world-and-life-view commitments has profound anthropological consequences: it is an expectation that denies the unity of human self-consciousness. Pushing against the agreement and organic unity that the soul and body constitute together, and within which the intellect, will, and feeling cooperate as the one person, it asks the Christian scientist to practice a form of cognitive dissonance. In Bavinck's view, the needs of the heart cannot be arbitrarily separated from the insights of the intellect. After all, the development of a world-and-life view means a person takes on philosophical and religious boundary-identifying ideas, which themselves become presuppositions—the very foundations of one's practice of life as a human. On account of this, it is neither just nor possible to shed such metaphysical commitments in the act of inductive investigation. As such, someone who is a Christian and a scientist must allow science the freedom it needs to discover without neglecting the authority of God's speech in God's world. This is the case "because all science is the translation of the thoughts that God has laid down in his works."[24] Although "pseudoscience

24. See p. 127, below.

can lead away from him, true science leads back to him. In him alone, who is the truth itself, do we find rest, as much for our understanding as for our heart."[25] There are a number of ways of speaking about Christian science that follow.

First, Bavinck states that "science owes to this gospel . . . the reality of an eternal, incorruptible truth."[26] Truth is not a mere subjective idea but rather is objective in God. Christianity supports science by rejecting skepticism in this regard. Further, it provides the presuppositions of both religion and science, namely, the creation of the world by the Godhead.

Second, Christian science, then, is a habitus of knowing that proceeds from the faith-knowledge of special revelation. It is science that "accepts special revelation":[27] "If God has communicated knowledge of himself in a special way, then it goes without saying that science must reckon with that, and failing to do so, it is guilty of disobedience and error."[28] The acceptance of special revelation is a question not of science but of religion, he argues. That means that Christian science proceeds on the basis of a world-and-life view whose boundaries are drawn by religion. For Bavinck, then, science either is biased against God or is for God, depending on its stance toward religion. And for a person who believes in the revelation

25. See p. 127, below.
26. See p. 186, below.
27. See p. 81, below.
28. See p. 81, below.

of God and in the creation by God's hand, it would be sinful to remove such faith from the judgments of scientific determination.

Third, science informed by Christianity understands that "religion and science . . . purity of heart and clarity of head . . . immoral life and ungodly doctrine are indubitably connected with one another."[29] The connection between religion and science is very close. For this reason, Christianity preserves both the religious and scientific personality of humanity and unifies the act of knowing.

Fourth, Bavinck argues, Christianity saves the sciences from positivism. It preserves the scientific nature of "literature, history, law, religion, and ethics, which together form the highest goods of humanity."[30] In this, the logic of the university is also preserved as a domain of organic knowledge.

Fifth, Christian science has the power both to make explicit that science proceeds on metaphysical assumption and to do so with precise claims about metaphysics itself.

> Recall but once that all science, including that of nature, rests upon metaphysical presuppositions and proceeds from general, self-establishing truths; . . . the reliability of the senses, the objective existence of the world, the truth of the laws of thinking, and the logical, ideal content of perceptible phenomena.[31]

29. See p. 86, below.
30. See p. 194, below.
31. See p. 131, below.

Christianity and Science is a prime example of Bavinck's long-standing view that for the Christian, the Logos is the ground of certainty in any act of scientific research. This, in turn, provides a basis for understanding the sciences as a single organism, with each field of science occupying one part of the organism that cannot be separated from the whole.

Sixth, Christian science allows the humanities to speak in more than simply a descriptive sense. It enables humanities to be treated as sciences, with objects to know and a power to speak prescriptively: "Everyone expects of these sciences that they will say what should count as religion, ethics, and law, for every person."[32] Positivism is a destructive force for ethics as a science, for example, necessarily reducing it to all manner of subjective constructs or a mere history without precept.

Finally, Christian science includes all the sciences and treats theology in particular as science. Bavinck's view is no less bold or provocative than this: Christianity is a blessing to science.[33] If science is defined exclusively by the empirical method, dogmatics is necessarily disallowed its scientific character. Yet, "a God who can in no sense be known is, in practical terms for us, the same as a God who does not exist."[34] If God cannot be known, then God cannot be served. Bavinck contends that those who

32. See p. 143, below.
33. See chap. 12, "The Blessing of Christianity for Science."
34. See p. 157, below.

have embraced the modernist (which is to say, empiricist) definition of science, and who treat religion and theology as merely historical or literary subjects, often assume that which they are disallowed to know: the existence of God. Further, as in his criticisms of positivism above, he argues that it is foolish for the modern scientist to suppose that theologians are dogmatic and proceed on the grounds of faith whereas science is scientific, open-ended, and proceeds on the ground of evidence. Both, he argues, are dogmatic and proceed from deeply ingrained intuitions. Bavinck makes an existential appeal on this front, that the religious person who says, "Whom have I in heaven but you?" cannot simply give up on faith because empiricist science declares God to be unknowable. "None who value religion and find their highest blessedness in fellowship with God can be neutral and objective regarding all that science is pleased to declare."[35] Rather, Bavinck writes, "[In response to] the science that is fashionable today, I call upon the science that has endured through the ages."[36] For Bavinck, then, Christian science assumes that the religious person who believes in the knowability of God must strive to unify head and heart, "faith and science."

At this juncture, it is important to note that Bavinck distinguishes the possibility of Christian science from religious science in a generic sense. Christianity does not

35. See p. 159, below.
36. See p. 160, below.

view religions as mere gradations of the same revelation but claims to be independent of all other religions. It claims knowledge of the triune God; of Christ as God and man, the messianic hope of the world; of the resurrected Christ in space and time. And so the Christian religion stands and falls on the confession of this special revelation. This particularity draws some boundaries for knowing. "If each religion is accompanied by a certain view of the world and humanity, of nature and history—which it always is—then through this it *binds* the whole of a person's life and also, specifically, [his] science."[37] There can be no "double truth" for the believer. Science and religion cannot walk side by side without touching. All faith, positivism included, brings religious ideas to bear on scientific conclusions. For the Christian, it is *Christian* godliness that is profitable for all things.

The Necessity of Christian Science

Finally, because faith aims toward knowledge—or, we might state differently, because faith seeks understanding—the emergence of Christian science is not merely a novel response to modernist positivism. Rather, it is a historic Christian practice, and a necessity of life in a fallen world. Without sin, Christian science would be wholly unnecessary. There would be no breach in the consciousness between religion and knowledge apart from the

37. See p. 180, below.

rupture-induced act of denying the word of God in the egocentricity of becoming like God in knowing good and evil. Sin damaged the self to the extent that knowledge of a fact no longer coincides with knowledge of God. For this reason, Bavinck offers the reader both an argument for the necessity of faith in doing science and a narrative of the emergence of Christian science in Christian history.

With regard to the emergence of Christian science in Christian history, Bavinck makes the magisterial claim that the apostles of Christ "planted the banner of truth in that world of unbelief and superstition."[38] He suggests that in the first century, skepticism and mysticism displaced the former highly ordered orientation toward systematic investigation (here he likely has Aristotle in view). Against that backdrop, in its unparalleled sweep of the Roman Empire, Christianity offered the world a religion of truth. While Christianity proved distinctively attractive because of the grace it offered (alongside its claim of a resurrected Messiah), Bavinck's account also makes the striking point that Christianity is a religion of grace precisely because it is first a commitment to truth. If the one God is truth, and his revelation in Jesus Christ is the unveiling of the truth, then all God does and says is truth. Christianity seeks not only to unveil truth but to make the first-order claim that God defines all truths, because God is truth and the author of essences. Thus, by

38. See p. 50, below.

the Spirit, "whoever believingly takes hold of this gospel is of the truth, is reborn through the truth, and is sanctified and freed [by it]. They are in the truth and the truth is in them."[39]

Bavinck's historical narrative then turns to focus on how this approach to truth broke through a culture of superstition in the "world of the Gentiles." The patristic fathers proved, as quoted above, that "Christianity was the true philosophy, and Christians were the real philosophers. They knew [*wisten*] reality in truth, they knew who God was, and now, equipped with this knowledge, they also had a different and better insight into the essence of the world, of nature and history."[40] Eventually, a positive approach had to be found with respect to the knowledge produced by the schools of the time, one that eschewed both the extreme of Tertullian's denial of the good of pagan philosophy and the Alexandrian exaltation of pagan philosophy. The temptation of Christians throughout history, Bavinck notes, has always been to one or the other: to separate faith from reason or to synthesize them in a syncretistic manner. It is the age-old tension between "world worship and world flight, culture idolatry and culture contempt, Enlightenment [*Aufklärung*] and pietism."[41] Despite this perennial struggle, Bavinck argues, a clear wisdom emerged, which he promotes in

39. See p. 51, below.
40. See p. 52, below.
41. See p. 55, below.

Christianity and Science and throughout his wider corpus: neither wholesale rejection nor acceptance of pagan insight.

Bavinck's own effort to avoid either error is thoroughly Augustinian, reflecting Augustine's general insight that truth is made known by the coherence of authority and reason within a framework of faith. For "science [*wetenschap*] can thus teach only a little, and that little only to a few. It does not know the way to the truth, for it does not know Christ, and thus it often leads to dead ends."[42] Although Bavinck certainly does regard Augustine's pairing of authority and reason to be at times dualistic, this Augustinian insight—that faith is a "gift of God" necessary for all knowledge, for all science—is valuable to him. Indeed, it leads to a further point regarding the necessity of the emergence of Christian science; namely, the logic of the necessity of faith as it relates to the possibility of knowledge. He explains this in the following remark:

> Faith strives toward knowledge [*kennis*] and is a means for knowing [*weten*]. That is already the case in the regular sciences, which, like the whole of human society, are built on and must proceed from faith. But this applies in particular with regard to that science which has the knowledge of God as its content. For this, the ground rule is given in the word of the prophet: "Unless you believe, you will

42. See p. 57, below.

> not understand" [Isa. 7:9]. We believe the truth of God precisely because we do not understand it, but by faith we are enabled to understand. Faith and science [*geloof en wetenschap*] thus stand next to one another in relationship like conception and birth, like tree and fruit, like work and wage; knowledge [*het weten*] is the fruit and wages of faith.[43]

While faith is critical to theology as science, faith is a requirement even in regular sciences like history, whose "facts" are dependent upon belief in human testimony, which is then a domain of knowledge that positivism logically excludes. All claims of knowledge depend upon philosophical determinations of the nature of knowledge. Epistemological self-consciousness is necessary for thoughtful science, but "it is not even possible to provide an epistemology [*Erkenntnisstheorie*] without metaphysics and philosophy."[44] While positivism stands on the presupposition that all knowledge is nothing but the determinations of sense perception, it fails to provide a rationale for the reliability of the senses and "the objectivity of the perceivable world." These assumptions, Bavinck argues, are not provable. "Here we merely point out that all scientific research assumes in advance and without proof the reliability of the senses and the objectivity of the perceivable world."[45] He even argues that the "reality

43. See p. 57, below.
44. See p. 92, below.
45. See p. 93, below.

of the world outside us is fixed by and for faith."[46] Those who doubt such things cannot be refuted by any arguments. When one faces them honestly, they can be driven either toward some form of skepticism or toward a faith position that all knowledge is preceded by trust in that which science cannot prove: perception, objectivity, and the possibility of knowledge itself. There is a necessity, Bavinck believes, in faith that precedes science because the outside world is a given by way of consciousness, not in itself. One cannot ever take a God's-eye view and perceive the phenomenal apart from personal consciousness.

Further, all manner of metaphysical assumptions are made in the act of scientific investigation: "Concepts, such as thing, property, cause, effect, law, condition, time, space, truth, falsehood, and more"[47] are assumed as realities despite their invisibility. Thus, faith is required to maintain objectivity. At its best, he reasons, this faith takes form and shape in Christian reason—a claim that requires treatment elsewhere in texts such as *Christian Worldview*. Nevertheless, the assumption of objectivity includes faith in the deepest ground of truthfulness in God.

For this reason, in Bavinck's view, it is appropriate to say that theology is both queen and servant of the sciences. As queen, theology offers the map of the terrain in which the sciences can move about freely. At the

46. See p. 93, below.
47. See p. 96, below.

same time, though, boundaries are necessary to protect the freedom of the other sciences from the overintrusion of theology. Theology can become guilty of the misuse of power and has been at various points in its history. The same is true of the other sciences. History is not short of examples of both theology and its fellow sciences overestimating their own distinctive reach and attempting to give answers for which they are not qualified.[48] Either implicitly or explicitly, this overreach sets distinctive sciences in competition—a historical backdrop that led to the dominance of empiricism in Bavinck's own context. His historical sketch portrays rationalism's own uneasy relationship to empiricism until the late nineteenth century surrendered thinking to radical empiricism, ignoring the basics of philosophical insight, not to mention theology. In his day, the elevation of empirical science into a de facto empiricism depended on a cultivated philosophical and theological naivete. It was possible, insofar as awareness of those sciences had been allowed to wither on the vine. In reply, Bavinck argued that every researcher brings all manner of "religious, moral, and philosophical convictions and is ruled by them to a greater or lesser degree."[49] This is even true of the radical positivists, whose conviction about the impossibility of metaphysical dogma is a dogmatic religious assertion in itself. Each party, in fact, proceeds on the implicit belief that the other party's prior

48. See p. 62, below.
49. See p. 83, below.

judgments are wrong. It is not that research simply carries on without such judgments.

Bavinck's claim is that every person must honestly deal with the assumed faith necessary even in the sensory and knowledge processes themselves. Facing this reality leads directly to the necessary relationship between metaphysics and science. One needs faith as a habitus, Bavinck supposed, because it is the means of disciplining reason, lest it fall by way of the pride of life. "Faith itself is an activity of the intellect, an act of thinking with consent, a deed of submission, of humility and lowliness, and as such it stands directly over against the pride and haughtiness of reason."[50] For this reason, Bavinck wrote that "on earth . . . we never rise above the standpoint of faith."[51]

Conclusion

In 1904, Bavinck saw the surfacing needs of the modern self, a fractured self, longing for an organic unity that arises in the consciousness of every human being. And so he issued a call and set forth an argument for the developing movement of "Christian science" in the European landscape to take shape all the more. All in all, he argued that the choice between science and religion is untenable. It is a false binary and, as such, is ill-suited to the realities of human life. Christian science is different. It allows the metaphysics of supernatural revelation to speak to the

50. See p. 57, below.
51. See p. 59, below.

causes and natures of things discovered as facts, and it makes no effort to disallow the freedom of the empirical sciences. Rather, it acknowledges the unity of the self in the activity of science and lets the holistic needs of human beings inform the boundaries and goal of the sciences. Christian science provides a ground for the objectivity of sense perception and for the reality of truth. It includes the claims of special revelation and reestablishes a place for theology as central in the organism of science, alongside and in service of the other disciplines.

Twelve decades on, some aspects of this text appear dated—most noticeably, for example, it was written in a historical context in which women had yet to gain admission to university education, as is reflected in this text's constant assumption that scientists are men;[52] and in the fleeting glimpses of colonial-era geopolitical anxiety that show Bavinck as a child of his time. Nonetheless, Bavinck's argument remains thought-provoking. It makes a clear case that Christianity is key to cultivating an approach to the life of the mind that is truly livable: it embraces the physical and the metaphysical; the material and the spiritual; creation, creature, and Creator. Consequently, it is an approach to the life of the mind that is deeply problematic to much scholarship and science in the early twenty-first century—among both scientific

52. Alongside this, of course, it should be noted that in the following year, Bavinck supported the admission of the first female student at the Free University of Amsterdam, Segrina 't Hooft (1883–1921), and later became a prominent advocate of women's education. See Eglinton, *Bavinck: A Critical Biography*, 237–38.

antireligionists and those whose religion prompts a deep aversion to science.

Some books set out to make their mark simply by ruffling feathers. *Christianity and Science* is no such book. It is more than simply an awkward presence. Rather, its argument reframes the issue of Christianity vis-à-vis the life of the mind in the light of more basic theological and anthropological questions: Who and what is God? And following this, what and who are we as creatures? Bavinck's discussion of those questions embeds and organizes the sciences within a framework, a grand narrative, and a shared telos; and in so doing, it grants them the gift of neighborliness. It lifts the eyes of each science beyond itself and tells each one, "You are not your own." In this, it gives the sciences precisely what the thin narrative of secular modernity—which offers little beyond a struggle for dominance in an immanent frame—cannot.

A Note on the Text

We have endeavored to provide the reader with a translation that is clear, accessible, accurate, and readable. Toward that end, where necessary, we have added illuminative words in order for particular sentences to make sense in English translation. These are always indicated in brackets. The original text makes numerous references to other figures and texts, some of which remain well known, while some others have faded into obscurity, despite the importance of their contributions in their own day. To open the text to contemporary readers, we have added references (including brief historical introductions) to these figures and technical terms in the footnotes, always indicating where a footnote is our own addition. Beyond that, we have retained Bavinck's own use of foreign language terms and quotes, providing English translations in each instance. Where knowledge of a particular Dutch term might help some readers appreciate the text with a greater degree of nuance, we have retained the original in brackets. Beyond that, our goal has been to have an otherwise inobtrusive role in bringing *Christianity and Science* to a non-Dutch readership. We acknowledge all mistakes and shortcomings as our own.

N. Gray Sutanto
James Eglinton
Cory C. Brock

1

Introduction

In recent years, an earnest and powerful striving to build science on the foundation of the Christian faith has been stirring. One can differ in appreciation of this fact, but its existence has risen far above all contradiction. The circle of those who are dissatisfied with the direction of leading contemporary science, in practice as in theory, is gradually increasing in size. There are many who desire something different, a different principle and a different method, for the practice of science.

There can also be no difference of opinion over the origin and character of this endeavor. For anyone who desires to see, it is clearly based on and directed by religious motivations. In the name of religion, for the sake of Christian truth, in order to bridge the chasm between the academy and [everyday] life, in the interest of the confession of the church, the scientific investigation of our time is judged in its principle, method, and purpose. Those who praise contemporary science cannot simply close their eyes to the religious character of this movement. Recently, Prof. Groenewegen of Leiden[1] gave witness to this in a notable way:

> The religious response has moved forward quietly, the public ecclesiastical-political response has followed. And now, finally, the scientific [community] must crown that effort, and, if possible, guard and confirm it. No one should underappreciate the original religious motivation of this powerful reactionary movement, which at times lends it a character worthy of praise.[2]

And so it is indeed. Christians, having gradually sunk into a deep sleep in the eighteenth century, suddenly experienced an awakening at the beginning of the [nineteenth] century, through which the Christian confessional and ecclesial consciousness was shaken out of its slumber. Looking around themselves, and discerning how much was neglected and taken for granted among them, the

1. Here Bavinck refers to Herman IJsbrand Groenewegen (1862–1930), professor of the philosophy of religion at the Remonstrant Seminary in Leiden.—Eds.

2. Herman Groenewegen, "Wetenschap of dogmatisme," *Theologisch tijdschrift* 37 (1903): 393. [Unless otherwise indicated, translations are our own.—Eds.]

believers once again arose and set to work. In the circles of the *Réveil*,[3] men devoted themselves mostly to evangelistic and philanthropic activities. The Secession[4] took up the reformation of the church and restored it to the foundation of the confession. On political terrain, the battle was mostly focused on the [fight for] Christian primary and secondary schools [*Christelijke volksschool*]. And slowly, the impression that the banner of the gospel must also be displayed over the world of science began to spread. Under all manner of misunderstandings and scorn, Van Oosterzee[5] took upon himself the defense of a science of faith. Chantepie de la Saussaye[6] bravely and definitively set his ethical method against empiricism. From then on, the battle against unbelieving science has continued to occupy an ever-more-principled standpoint. The Reformed Churches [*Gereformeerde Kerken*][7] tasked the Theological School

3. The *Réveil* was a nineteenth-century Protestant revival movement that began in Switzerland and spread into France, Germany, and the Netherlands.—Eds.

4. Bavinck is referring to the Secession (*Afscheiding*) of 1834, in which a group of churches seceded from the Dutch Reformed Church (*Nederlandse Hervormde Kerk*). The denomination formed in this secession eventually became known as the Christian Reformed Church (*Christelijke Gereformeerde Kerk*) and was the denomination into which Bavinck was born.—Eds.

5. Johannes Jacobus van Oosterzee (1817–1882), a Dutch theologian, pastor, and poet, was professor of biblical and practical theology at the University of Utrecht when, in 1876, the newly passed Higher Education Act required academic theologians to discontinue teaching theology and instead begin teaching religious studies.—Eds.

6. [Daniel] Chantepie de la Saussaye (1818–1874), a Dutch theologian and professor at the University of Groningen, is regarded as the father of the "ethical theology" movement—Eds.

7. Here Bavinck refers to the Reformed Churches in the Netherlands (*Gereformeerde Kerken in Nederland*), a denomination formed in the Union of Churches (1892) that merged the Christian Reformed Church and the *Nederduitse Gereformeerde Kerk (Dolerende)*, which had been led out of the Dutch Reformed Church (*Nederlandse Hervormde Kerk*) by Abraham Kuyper in 1886—Eds.

in Kampen[8] with the duty of forming future ministers of the word through the scientific study of theology and the practical preparation for sacred ministry. The Free University of Amsterdam set as its goal the practice of science and the [provision of] education for all manner of callings in life, in accordance with Reformed principles. We are already so far advanced in our homeland that a bill for the recognition of special professorial chairs[9] and the degrees [awarded by] private universities[10] was submitted to the House of Representatives, and was accepted with 56 votes for and 41 votes against. However weak it may be, a revival of Christian science can be seen, and that fills the heart with hope for the future.

This phenomenon in our homeland is all the more remarkable and is gaining significance because it is not an isolated occurrence. Elsewhere, too, signs of such a scientific movement can be perceived. Namely, among Roman Christians, especially after the encyclical by Pope Leo XIII on August 4, 1879, recommended the study of Thomas, a zeal to practice science in accordance with his

8. Bavinck refers to the Theologische School in Kampen (later the Theologische Universiteit Kampen), the seminary established by the Christian Reformed Churches in 1854.—Eds.

9. The "special professorial chairs" (*bijzondere leerstoelen*) are professorial positions at universities that are endowed by external organizations rather than paid for by the universities themselves, and with a remit for research and teaching that is set by the external funder. The *bijzondere leerstoel* role first became legal in the Netherlands in 1905 and was introduced by Abraham Kuyper.—Eds.

10. Bavinck has in view the distinction between "public" (*openbare*) and "private" (*bijzondere*) universities. Public universities were established by the state, whereas private universities were founded by private individuals or groups—the Free University of Amsterdam, established by Abraham Kuyper in 1880, was one such example. In that period, public universities were funded by the state, whereas private universities were not.—Eds.

principles was awakened, the depth of which should put believing Protestants to shame. There are hardly any scientific subjects that do not include his skilled exponents and representatives. In foundational scholarly works and narrow, detailed research, the Roman foundation is applied to the entire terrain of science. Logic and psychology, metaphysics and theology, history and literature, jurisprudence and sociology are practiced in such a way by them that the opponent must reckon with their work. And although the antithesis [between Protestant and Roman Catholic], which is so clearly again manifested in the work of Denifle on Luther,[11] should in no way be ignored or weakened, their [Catholics'] scientific studies can be consulted nevertheless with great profit by all who still stand on the foundation of the universal, indubitable Christian faith.

We may even go a step further and bring this resurgence of a Christian practice of science in connection with a succession of phenomena, all of which show that positivism's days are numbered. The slogan "back to Kant" has lost its charm for many. The philosophy of Hume and Comte increasingly gives way to that of Leibniz and Hegel. Everywhere, there is a perceptible return from empiricism to idealism. Following the supreme rule

11. Bavinck is alluding to the work of Heinrich Denifle (1844–1905), an Austrian Roman Catholic paleographer and historian who published works severely criticizing Martin Luther. See Henrich Denifle, *Luther und Luthertum in der ersten Entwicklung quelienmässig darstellt* (Mainz: Kirchheim, 1904); *Luther in rationalistischer und christlicher Beleuchtung* (Mainz: Kirchheim, 1904).—Eds.

of understanding, feeling has retaken its rights, theory makes way for life, and rationalism stands aside for the romantic. The mystical makes its entry into art. In natural science we behold a turnaround that had seemed impossible for decades. At that time [during the zenith of the enlightenment], materialism was held to be the highest wisdom, and the mechanistic explanation of the world was deemed the only scientific one. Now, we witness how many of the most exceptional naturalists are returning from mechanism to dynamism, from materialism to the energetic [explanation of the world], from causality to teleology, from atheism to theism. After the thirst for facts is initially quenched, hunger for the knowledge of the origin and goal, for the cause and essence of the things above, resurfaces.[12]

Naturally, this remarkable reversal in science also benefits religion. The time is not far behind us when natural science, history, and philosophy all alike questioned their reason for existence. For a few years, Haeckel[13] believed that he had put [this questioning] to death in his *The Riddle of the Universe*,[14] and that he had cleared up the

---

12. Compare Ludwig Stein, *Der Sinn des Daseins: Streifzüge eines Optimisten durch die Philosophie der Gegenwart* (Tübingen: Mohr, 1904), 84; Willem van der Vlugt in the *Tweede Kamer*, February 26, 1904, *Proceedings*, 1391.

13. Ernst Haeckel (1834–1919), a German naturalist, eugenicist, social Darwinist, and philosopher.—Eds.

14. Ernst Haeckel, *Die Welträthsel: Gemeinverständliche Studien über Monistische Philosophie* (Bonn: Strauss, 1899); English title: *The Riddle of the Universe at the Close of the Nineteenth Century* (Cambridge: Cambridge University Press, 2011). In Haeckel's account, the "world riddle" concerned the search for a single answer to the questions What is the nature of the physical universe? and What is the nature of human thinking?—Eds.

dogmas of God, the soul, and immortality for good. But the reception of this work, which came from the scientific circles, shows that thought here had already turned in another direction. The metaphysical need lies too deep in human nature to be silenced in the long run. Not only is this recoupment—which people seek as religion in all manner of paths, in spiritism and theosophy, in humanitarianism and the idolization of culture, in Buddhism and Islam—a clear proof of the metaphysical's indispensability, but there is in broad circles a desire to detect a more or less positive Christian faith. Humanity is tired of doubt and uncertainty. Even among modern theologians, men who insist on a confession and dogmatics, on ecclesial organization and liturgical unity, arise.[15] Faith in such a highly self-conscious modern culture has been shaken. Exact science has not delivered what men like Renan had expected from it in their youthful hubris. And so, one returns to the formerly scorned religion, by no means always in true repentance but nevertheless in despondent doubt.

An era that manifests such signs is not unfavorable for the practice of science in a Christian spirit. It is thus

15. A. Bruining, "Het aggressief karacter van het vrijzinnig godsienstig," in *Religion and Liberty: Addresses and Papers at the Second International Council of Unitarian and Other Liberal Religious Thinkers and Workers*, ed. P. H. Hugenholtz Jr. (Leiden: Brill, 1904), 168–78; S. Cramer, "Does Liberal Christianity Want Organizing in Special Churches and Congregations?," in Hugenholtz, *Religion and Liberty*, 227, 237; Bruining, "Over de methode van onze dogmatiek," *Teyler's theologisch tijdschrift* 1 (1903); also Prof. Groenewegen, Prof. Knappert, Dr. J. Van der Berg, Rev. Groot, Rev. Feenstra et al. in the gathering of modern theologians and in the weekly *De Hervorming*.

important, for oneself and others, for friend and foe, to give a clearer account of what should be meant by such a practice of science. It cannot be done with the clichés of reactionary dogmatism. Whoever has a sense of the power of religious convictions, whoever knows the driving power of principles that take root in life and, with this, knows to point out the signs of times, cannot be guilty of underestimating such an earnest and powerful movement, much less of taking an indifferent attitude toward it. Believing and unbelieving, Christian and positivistic views of science stand diametrically opposed to each other. Compromise is not possible here; rather [there is] a duty to make a definite choice. However, to that end, a clearer understanding of the unique features of both views is an indispensable requirement.

2

How the Concept of a Christian Science Emerged

When Christianity entered the world through the preaching of the apostles more than eighteen centuries ago, it discovered not only a powerful state and a well-ordered society but also a highly developed culture. And yet, traces of decline and dissolution were already present there. In particular, the heyday of science was already long gone. The power of thought [*denkkracht*] had been exhausted and was no longer capable of creating systems. Together, eclecticism and syncretism studied what good could be found in different movements. Mysticism sought a new path to the kingdom of knowledge through contemplation and asceticism. And, whether in doubt or in mockery, skepticism uttered the question "What is truth?"

The apostles of Jesus planted the banner of truth in that world of unbelief and superstition. After all, the Christian religion is not merely the religion of grace. It is also the religion of truth. It is the one because it is the other. This is why Holy Scripture frequently speaks of the truth—its essence and worth are put forth in the clearest light through all of revelation. God himself is the truth, in distinction from all creatures, which have no peace in themselves, [for he is] truly and essentially God; he stands in contrast especially with human beings, who lie, and with idols, which are nothingness and vanity. And because God is pure truth, only light without darkness, it follows that whatever comes from him—his words and works, his paths and ways, his rights and commandments—is truth. Whatever he does stands on justice and truth as on immovable pillars. Specifically, as the highest and fullest revelation of God, Christ is called the way, the truth, and the life. He is indeed the Word, who was in the beginning with God and was himself God, the image of the invisible God, the radiance of his glory and express image of his independence, in whom the fullness of God dwells bodily, and all treasures of wisdom and knowledge are hidden. What no one could do, he has done. No one has ever seen God, but the only begotten Son, the one who is in the Father's bosom, has declared him to us. He has revealed his name and made the truthful one known to us. And he lived up to this declaration of the name of the Father to the point of death; he made a good profession under Pontius Pilate; he is the faithful witness, the firstborn of the dead. His gospel, then, is also the word of truth. And so that we would believe and understand this gospel, he has sent the Holy Spirit, who, as the Spirit of truth, leads us into all truth and bears witness to it and seals it in our hearts. Whoever believingly takes hold of this gospel is of the truth, is reborn through the truth, and is sanctified and freed [by it]. They are in the truth and the truth is in them. They speak and do the truth and even risk their lives for their confession.

The work that went out from this gospel of truth into the heathen world was powerful. The apostles arose in a society undermined by doubt and unbelief. A multitude of men and women soon emerged with and after them—[men and women] who were convinced in the depth of their souls that an absolute, full, and trustworthy truth existed, that this was available and knowable for everyone by way of faith, and that it gifted life, freedom, and salvation to everyone who received it in obedience. No words can express all that was bound up in this [transformation]. A feeling takes over the heart as in a castaway plucked from the waves, who feels solid ground beneath his feet again. Doubt makes way for certainty, fear for trust, and angst for [hitherto] unknown happiness.

The writings of the first Christians provide an overabundance of proof of this. They spoke out of a firm awareness that in the gospel of Jesus Christ they possessed the truth, and that with that treasure they were richer than all the thinkers of that age. Because the world with all its wisdom had not known God, God was pleased to save all who believed through the foolishness of preaching. God had done away with the wisdom of the wise, and he had made nothing the understanding of the prudent. The wisdom of the world turned out to be foolishness and idle philosophy, and the gospel revealed and demonstrated itself to be the power and wisdom of God. So speaks the apostle Paul, who grounded his honor in taking all the thoughts and intentions of the heart captive to the obedience of Christ, and so spoke every believer after him. Christianity was the true philosophy, and Christians were the real philosophers. They knew [*wisten*] reality in truth, they knew who God was, and now, equipped with this knowledge, they also had a different and better insight into the essence of the world, of nature and history. A high self-consciousness was inherent in the first Christian congregations. They were the people of God, the oldest people of the earth, for whose sake the world was created, that now in the administration of the new covenant all opposition between Jew and Gentile, Greek and Barbarian is resolved in a higher unity [for those] who have been called to a worldwide task and with Christ are heirs over all things.[1]

1. Adolf von Harnack, *Die Mission und die Ausbreitung des Christenthums in den ersten drei Jahrhunderten* (Leipzig: Hinrichs, 1902), 161, 177.

Animated by this conviction, these Christians formed an independent community with an idiosyncratic world of thought [*gedachtenkring*] and way of life, with an idiosyncratic world-and-life view. They stood antithetically against the world and had little in common with it. They fought idolatry and idol worship, demonic faith and sorcery, the deification of man and emperor worship, the theaters and games; they went against all of the thinking, living, and striving of their time. But they could not stay within this antithesis indefinitely. Paul had already indicated that if believers wanted to break away from all community with unbelievers, they would have to leave the world itself—the impossibility of which was felt ever more deeply [in the passage of time]. It came to light fully when not only male and female slaves but also lords and ladies, merchants and tradesmen, civil servants and politicians, artists and philosophers came to the Christian faith. The practice of abstaining [from the world] was no longer viable. A positive arrangement had to be found.

The same need soon arose in the domain of science. Here it was particularly difficult to find the right way through the labyrinth of systems and schools. It was little wonder that many went astray and deviated to the right or to the left. The North African school, represented by Tertullian, stood on one side; pagan literature, so he said, has no worth for life and no use for Christianity, for it is proved to be foolishness before God. Philosophy is an idle, worldly science, which the Christian can neither teach nor practice. What do Athens and Jerusalem, the academy and the church, heretics and Christians, have in common? We have no more need for philosophy after Jesus Christ and no more [use for] investigation after the gospel. If we believe, we want nothing more above that.

In the opposite direction stood the Alexandrian school, with its teachers Clement[2] and Origen.[3] These saw a lower rung of science [as inherent] within [Christian] faith and thus strove to elevate faith toward knowledge and thereby to complete it. Just as the progression from paganism to Christianity was a first "healing change" [*heilzame verandering*], so was the development from Christian faith to science a second. For faith is the standpoint of fear, but knowledge is the standpoint of love; faith is a summary of that which is most necessary, but knowledge is the firm demonstration of what is believed. Now, in order to bring this faith over to knowledge, on the one hand, pagan philosophy became so highly elevated as the fruit of the Logos that it came close to [being deemed part of] Christianity itself; and on the other hand, especially through the allegorical interpretation of Scripture, Christian truth became so generalized that it could be joined harmonically to pagan wisdom. And so a typical mediation theology [*bemiddlings-theologie*] emerged,

2. Titus Flavius Clemens, otherwise known as Clement of Alexandria (150–215), an early Christian theologian and philosopher.—Eds.

3. Origen of Alexandria (185–253), an early Christian theologian.—Eds.

which erased the opposites and did no justice to divine truth or human science.

Both of these directions have always had their interpreters and defenders in the Christian world. In every age, there have been those who have leaned to one side or another: world worship and world flight, culture idolatry and culture contempt, Enlightenment [*Aufklärung*] and pietism, rationalism and mysticism constantly trade places in history. And yet, it is incorrect to identify either one of these directions with Christian truth. The assertion of Hatch and Harnack that Christian dogma and Christian theology is a fruit of the marriage between Greek philosophy and the original gospel is untenable.[4] Without doubt, classical science has rendered its services to theology, and the development of church and theology, according to the judgment of Reformed principles, has by no means been pure and infallible. But this acknowledgment is still vastly different from the claim that [Christian] dogma as such is the work of the Greek mind on the base level of the gospel.

Warned by the one-sidedness of the North African and Alexandrian schools, Christian theologians quickly and clearheadedly gave an account of the position that Christian truth occupied against pagan science. They

4. Here Bavinck alludes to the German higher critical theologian Adolf von Harnack (1851–1930) and his English counterpart Edwin Hatch (1835–1889). See Edwin Hatch, *The Influence of Greek Ideas and Usages on the Early Church* (London: Williams and Norgate, 1891); Adolf von Harnack, *History of Dogma*, vol. 1 (London: Williams and Norgate, 1894), 57.—Eds.

soon came to the insight that it was to be neither wholly rejected nor wholly accepted. According to the words of Paul, everything here was to be tested, but only that which was good, retained. For this reason, they loved the image that the people of God were allowed to enrich themselves with the treasures of Egypt, and Solomon was allowed to construct his temple with help of the builders of Hiram and the cedars of Lebanon.[5]

It was particularly Augustine[6] who so precisely identified the path to be followed and thereby drew the baselines for a Christian practice of science. From youth he was consumed by a burning love for the truth. He was not satisfied with the search for the truth as Lessing[7] was later; rather, he was concerned with the truth itself. After he had sought the truth in vain among the Manichaeans[8] and the skeptics,[9] in Plato[10] and Plotinus,[11] he finally found it through the church in the gospel of Christ. And from then on, he set forth two epistemic sources of the truth next to one another: authority and reason. Philosophy is not in a position to make known the truth we need,

---

5. Joseph Mausbach, *Christenthum und Weltmoral* (Munster: Aschendorf, 1897).

6. Augustine of Hippo (354–430), the North African Christian theologian and philosopher.—Eds.

7. Here Bavinck refers to the German philosopher Gotthold Lessing (1729–1781). Lessing is best known for his insistence that there is a "broad ugly ditch" between history and eternal truths.—Eds.

8. The Manichaeans were followers of a dualistic ancient religion based on the teachings of the Parthian prophet Mani (216–274)—Eds.

9. The academic skeptics were a movement in ancient Greek philosophy that insisted that humans lacked the capacity to grasp truth.—Eds.

10. Plato (428/427 or 424/423–348/347 BC), the ancient Greek philosopher.—Eds.

11. Plotinus (204/205–270), a Neoplatonic philosopher.—Eds.

not so much because the faculty of reason is so weak and limited but because the human being is so corrupted by sin. One's pride, one's self-love in particular, stands in the way of the discovery of truth. Science [*wetenschap*] can thus teach only a little, and that little only to a few. It does not know the way to the truth, for it does not know Christ, and thus it often leads to dead ends. Hence, in authority, God has given yet another epistemic source of knowledge. Because we are ensnared in the earthly and are inclined against the eternal, faith is necessary as a "temporary medicine" [*tijdelijk medicijn*] to give us knowledge of the truth. That faith is a gift of God. He works with his Spirit in our hearts and there moves our wills in such a way that we believe wholly willingly; and this cannot be otherwise, for no one can believe against his will. But that faith itself is an activity of the intellect, an act of thinking with consent, a deed of submission, of humility and lowliness, and as such it stands directly over against the pride and haughtiness of reason.

Now, that faith certainly already presupposes some knowledge of the object of faith. For otherwise there could be no talk of faith. But this knowledge, which precedes faith, only carries a provisional character and is not knowledge in the actual sense. Of much more significance is the knowledge that follows and flows out of faith. For faith strives toward knowledge [*kennis*] and is a means for knowing [*weten*]. That is already the case in the regular sciences, which, like the whole of human society, are built on and must proceed from faith. But this applies in particular with regard to that science which has the knowledge of God as its content. For this, the ground rule is given in the word of the prophet: "Unless you believe, you will not understand" [Isa. 7:9]. We believe the truth of God precisely because we do not understand it, but by faith we are enabled to understand. Faith and science [*geloof en wetenschap*] thus stand next to one another in relationship like conception and birth, like tree and fruit, like work and wage; knowledge [*het weten*] is the fruit and wages of faith.

Starting from here, Augustine roused himself and others to consider this truth, which we already possess by faith, also in light of reason. God does not despise reason, which in any case is his gift. Pagan science, however much it erred, nonetheless saw a shadow of truth; it drew from God's revelation in nature and reason. And Christians may, and indeed must, profit from the truth that is present in that pagan science; it is fitting that they appropriate it as their rightful property. In accordance with this, Augustine exerted all his cognitive powers to demonstrate rationally the reality of ideas, the existence of God, the spiritual nature of the soul, and even the doctrine of the Trinity. And yet, he was not of the opinion that all that was already believed here on earth could already be known. That was not even the case with the ordinary sciences. Many things remain the object of faith: for example, the facts of history, all of which rest on human testimony. Only with regard to the so-called eternal truths—which are dealt with in logic, mathesis,[12] etc.—is science possible in the strict sense. But other than that, we never rise above faith, and especially not in theology. What I know [*weet*], I believe; but I do not know [*weet*] everything that I believe. Often, we can only go as far as to show that it is not foolish to believe in revelation but that it is indeed foolish the accept the opposite. Here on earth, therefore, we never rise above the standpoint of faith. Only in heaven does faith receive the knowledge of sight as its reward.[13]

---

12. Bavinck is referring to the *mathesis universalis*, a hypothetical universal science modeled on mathematics by the likes of Leibniz and Descartes. See Chikara Sasaki, *Descartes's Mathematical Thought* (Dordrecht: Springer, 2013), 194.—Eds.

13. Cf. Heinrich Ritter, *Geschichte der christlichen Philosophie*, vol. 2 (Hamburg: Perthes, 1841), 189; Albert Stöckl, *Geschichte der christlichen Philosophie zur Zeit der Kirchenväter* (Mainz: Kirchheim, 1891), 302; and Theodor Gangauf, *Metaphysische Psychologie des heiligen Augustinus* (Augsburg, 1852), 31.

3

Defects That Clung to Christian Science

The edifice of Christian science was built on these foundations. It remained standing for centuries, and its grandeur still enchants the attentive observer. And yet, there were defects that clung to this human effort that became more visible over time. Science, as it was practiced in the Middle Ages and afterward also in Protestant Christianity until about the middle of the eighteenth century, suffered from one-sidedness and shortcomings, which could not but lead to deterioration and decline.

First, although faith and reason were initially united most closely and harmoniously, they were soon torn apart and placed loosely side by side. Each was accompanied by its own set of truths. There were supernatural truths, which were accepted on the basis of authority. Alongside these were natural truths, which could be found by reason. With the former, only faith was possible; and with the latter, pure and accurate knowledge [*weten*] was accessible. The consequence of this was that these two truths stood side by side separately, and finally even led some to believe not that the truth itself was one but, rather, that something true in philosophy could be false in theology, and vice versa. Even though people mostly recoiled from this dangerous consequence, the separation, the juxtaposition, nevertheless became a cause of rivalry; rivalry led to strife, and strife usually caused reason to be silenced in the name of revelation, or revelation to be combatted and rejected in the name of reason.

A second defect was that for a variety of causes, the science of that era became much too involved in theology, and did so one-sidedly into dogmatics. With the help of philosophy, theology had been the first [science] to develop in the Christian age. In itself, the expression that philosophy is the handmaiden of theology contains nothing dishonoring to science. After all, it was and remains [science] that grants the truth of God the formal means of taking up a position on scientific terrain. Gradually, however, this expression was understood and applied in such a way that science was robbed of all freedom of movement and could be nothing but the obedient servant of theology.

And [theology], misusing its power, gradually expanded its territory. It did not limit itself to the exposition of the revealed knowledge of God but took up into itself all sorts of sciences, such as psychology, cosmology, metaphysics, and more, and gave answers to all questions—possible and impossible—providing an entire world-and-life view.

Alongside this was a third defect, which lay in the neglect of empiricism. The theory was pure; Roman Catholic and Protestant theologians have never taught otherwise than that all intellectual knowledge begins with sense perception. When Bacon referred back to experience as the source of knowledge, he was not saying anything new in theory.[1] But as is often the case, it was also the case here that life did not correspond to doctrine. Living under the naive assumption that the men of antiquity had sufficiently consulted sense perception, the scholastics drew the material for the various sciences from the works of the ancients, instead of drawing the fresh water of knowledge from the sources themselves. Philosophy was studied from Aristotle,[2] medicine from Hippocrates,[3] mathematics from Euclid,[4] Latin grammar from Donatus,[5] rhetoric

1. To a greater or lesser extent, the method that Bacon recommended for the study of nature was already used by his great contemporaries Tycho Brahe, Kepler, Galileo, and others. Joseph de Maistre therefore said that Bacon was a barometer "who announced the beautiful weather, and that because he announced it, it is believed that he made it" [der das schöne Wetter verkündigte, und weil er es verkündigte, glaubt man, er habe es gemacht]. Alois Schmid, *Erkenntnislehre*, vol. 2 (Freiburg: Herder, 1890), 291.
2. Aristotle (384–322 BC), the ancient Greek philosopher.—Eds.
3. Hippocrates (460–370 BC), the ancient Greek physician.—Eds.
4. Euclid, the ancient Greek mathematician and logician.—Eds.
5. Aelius Donatus, the fourth-century Roman grammarian.—Eds.

from Quintilian,[6] music from Boethius,[7] and theology from Lombard.[8] Science became a study of books. People forgot to see through their own eyes. [We should take care] not to attribute too much to this defect in scholasticism. After all, [it is not the case that] everyone can do everything, and everything has its proper time. For all kinds of practical and technical reasons, the study of nature, as we now know it, was not possible in centuries gone by. But still, the neglect of experience was a defect that would avenge itself in the long run.

The reaction [to this neglect] had already begun at the transition from the Middle Ages to the modern era. This new era not only was ushered in by the Reformation but was just as much prepared by the rise of the free bourgeoisie, the Renaissance, the awakening of the natural sciences, the discovery of America, the development of trade and shipping, and more. While each of these phenomena and events bears its own particular character, together they are also revelations of a new spirit, which had outgrown the discipline of scholasticism and hierarchy. They have in common the thirst for freedom, the recognition of the natural. This was so because in the Middle Ages, the natural was externally suppressed, but was not internally sanctified. Hence, in the end it threw off its chains and retook its rights.

---

6. Marcus Fabius Quintilianus (ca. 35–ca.100), the Roman rhetorician.—Eds.
7. Anicius Manlius Severinus Boethius (ca. 480–524), a Roman philosopher.—Eds.
8. Peter Lombard (ca. 1096–1160), a medieval scholastic theologian.—Eds.

Among all of these weighty events, the Reformation distinguished itself for its religious-ethical motives and purposes. It did not stand up for the emancipation of mankind but joined the fight against Rome for the freedom of the Christian. But the power, namely, that of the Renaissance, that emerged independently alongside it was not inclined to let the Reformation lay down the law. And thus, the religious Reformation was quickly stopped in its tracks and, to its own detriment, had to limit itself to church and theology, while alongside it science increasingly began to consider independence as its ideal. Emancipation became the driving force in its striving: emancipation, in the first place, from the church and its confession, but also from Christianity and Scripture. For a while, a solution was cautiously sought in separation. Faith and science would live at peace with one another after a proper division of property, and leave each other undisturbed. Faith had to confine itself to theology and the church, and science had to refrain from assaulting dogma. In the first period after the Reformation, science in no way wanted to be completely unbelieving. It left theology alone, itself having also started from a dogma—though not an ecclesiastical dogma, but a metaphysical and rationalistic one. The divisions in the religious and ecclesial domains, which could be seen soon after the Reformation, encouraged this direction and drove many back to the underlying general, natural truths behind the differences. In religion, morality, and law, the sum of rational truths was elevated as a foundation and was accepted as a guide. In Comte's[9] terms, science transitioned from a theological to a metaphysical phase. While formerly everything was understood as the act of a personal God, people became accustomed to what Ludwig Stein[10] calls "competent" [*zuständliche*] thinking,[11] and saw in everything the operation of abstract essences and natural laws. Descartes[12] proceeded from fixed, innate concepts. Spinoza[13] handled the whole world as a geometric problem, whereby one thing necessarily followed the other. Leibniz[14] constructed the universe from the harmonious cooperation of metaphysical powers. Even the French Revolution bore a dogmatic character and was led by abstract principles of rights and freedoms.

This rationalistic dogmatism collapsed under the critique of the Königsberg philosopher Immanuel Kant. In order to make room for faith, he abolished knowledge [*weten*] of the metaphysical realm. Like Bacon,[15] he proposed a distinction between believing and knowing [*gelooven en weten*]. He conjectured this not only for the sake of peace; in principle he also tried to derive it as necessary [in view of] human cognitive function. By virtue

9. Auguste Comte (1789–1857), a French positivist philosopher.—Eds.

10. Ludwig Stein (1859–1930), a Hungarian-Swiss rabbi, philosopher, and sociologist.—Eds.

11. Ludwig Stein, *Der Sinn des Daseins: Streifzüge eines Optimisten durch die Philosophie der Gegenwart* (Tübingen: Mohr, 1904), 88.

12. René Descartes (1596–1650), the French philosopher, mathematician, and scientist. In the original text, Bavinck used the Latinized form Cartesius.—Eds.

13. Baruch Spinoza (1632–1677), the Dutch Jewish philosopher.—Eds.

14. Gottfried Wilhelm Leibniz (1646–1716), the German polymath.—Eds.

15. Francis Bacon (1561–1626), the English philosopher whose works influenced the scientific revolution.—Eds.

of the organization of the cognitive faculties, knowledge [*het weten*] was limited to the sense-perceptible world; behind and above it, though, an unknown land—a *terra incognita*—stretched out, [a land] that offered a haven of refuge and hiding place to faith. Kant achieved this fundamental and radical separation, however, by starting from a loaded, unproven apriorism, which asserted that our cognitive faculty was accompanied by synthetic a priori judgments and thus carried within itself the general and necessary categories of the phenomenal world. Neglecting the criticism and dualism [found] in Kant's system, the subsequent speculative philosophy of Fichte,[16] Schelling,[17] and Hegel[18] latched on to this apriorism and built upon it. If the "I" could be the creator of the phenomenal world, there was no longer any objection to making it absolute and then exalting it to be the principle of all that exists. Kant's "epistemic-theoretical" [*erkenntnisstheoretische*] idealism thus developed into an ethical idealism by Fichte, an aesthetic idealism by Schelling, and a logical idealism or pantheism by Hegel.

Whatever high place this idealism ascribed to science and the university came not only from Kant's "The Conflict of the Faculties" [*Der Streit der Fakultäten*],[19] in

16. Johann Gottlieb Fichte (1762–1814), a German idealist philosopher.—Eds.

17. Friedrich Wilhelm Joseph Schelling (1775–1854), a German idealist philosopher.—Eds.

18. Georg Wilhelm Friedrich Hegel (1770–1831), a German idealist philosopher.—Eds.

19. Here Bavinck refers to Kant's argument for the necessity of free and open argument in the university setting and his criticism of repression of argument in the context of Prussian censorship. See Immanuel Kant, "The Conflict of the Faculties,"

which only the philosophical faculty could be described as truly serving science. [Alongside this] it came to light even more clearly in the "Plan for an Establishment of Higher Learning to Be Founded in Berlin" [*Plan einer zu Berlin zu errichtenden höheren Lehranstalt*], which Fichte produced in the year 1807.[20] There he developed the idea that the universities form an indispensable ingredient of national education and have the specific task of education through science and for science. In order to realize this ambition, they must be completely isolated "from the general mass of commercial and philistinic Bourgeoisie"[21] [*von der allgemeinen Masse des gewerbetreibenden und dumpfgeniessenden Bürgerthums*]; they must not be tormented by the concerns of earthly existence, nor burdened by having to take care of practical cares. They have only to devote themselves to the holy task of science and to focus all of their attention there. Just as all life self-propagates, their ultimate calling is to transmit science from generation to generation, and to that end, [their calling is] to cultivate men for this purpose, who themselves will then go on to practice science. The universities must not be schools to educate [the

in *Religion and Rational Theology*, trans. and ed. Allen Wood and George di Giovanni (Cambridge: Cambridge University Press, 1996), 233–328.—Eds.

20. Here Bavinck refers to Fichte's "Deductive Plan for an Establishment of Higher Learning to Be Founded in Berlin" ("Deducierter Plan einer zu Berlin zu errichtenden höheren Lehranstalt," published in J. G. Fichte, *Sämtliche Werke*, vol. 3 (Berlin: Verlag von Veit, 1845), 97–204.—Eds.

21. For a more extensive interaction with Fichte's plan, see Herman Bavinck, "The Teaching Office," in *On Theology: Herman Bavinck's Academic Orations*, ed. and trans. Bruce Pass (Leiden: Brill, 2021), 100.—Eds.

general public], but rather are seminaries for professors. In this way, Fichte wanted to elevate the university to the center of all understanding and knowing [*weten en kennen*], as the workplace of the divine idea of humankind; to him, it was "the most Sacred possession of the human race, the visible presentation of the unity of the world, as the appearance of God and God himself" [*das Heiligste, was das Menschengeschlecht besitzt, die sichtbare Darstellung der Einheit der Welt, als der Erscheinung Gottes und Gottes selbst*].[22]

Whatever exalted sense may now pervade this conception of science and university, it is fortunate that it was not applied in practice. The University of Berlin, for which Fichte designed his plan, was organized completely differently. Wilhelm von Humboldt,[23] who developed its statutes, did not construe it according to philosophical categories, but rather reckoned with reality and prescribed that it would also form servants for church and state. And this was not all. Through its aprioristic constructions of the world at large, German idealism's overconfident speculation soon disappointed the expectation that it would solve the problems of life. And when at the same time the historical sense was awakened and

22. Cf. Kuno Fischer, *Geschichte der neuern Philosophie*, 10 vols. (Heidelberg: Winter, 1897–1904), 5:768–71; Martin von Nathusius, *Das Wesen der Wissenschaft und ihre Anwendung auf die Religion: Empirische Grundlegung für die theologische Methodologie* (Leipzig: Hinrichs, 1885), 40.

23. Wilhelm von Humboldt (1767–1835), a Prussian philosopher, linguist, and diplomat. He founded the University of Berlin, which was later renamed the Humboldt University of Berlin in his honor.—Eds.

the study of nature was undertaken with new courage, a passion for reality arose, which silenced all metaphysics, theology, and philosophy and ensured that the inductive method had exclusive sovereignty. In Germany, to the extent that people recoiled from materialism, they went back to Kant's criticism; in France, the philosophy of Victor Cousin[24] gave way to that of August Comte; in England, John Stuart Mill[25] stood foursquare on the empirical standpoint; and everywhere, this conception of science as the only true [explanation] was gradually proclaimed, which exhibits its most familiar characteristic in the demand for absolute "presuppositionlessness" [*Voraussetzungslosigkeit*].

24. Victor Cousin (1792–1867), a French philosopher whose "eclecticism" attempted to hold together elements of German idealism and Scottish common sense realism.—Eds.

25. John Stuart Mill (1806–1873), an English philosopher and political economist. Mill's work was influential in the development of classical liberalism.—Eds.

4

Positive Science

According to this view, science had previously gone through a theological and metaphysical phase but has now transitioned, and should appropriately transition, into this positive period. Just as, according to sociological law, a human being is a theologian in infancy and a metaphysician in youth, and then a physicist in adulthood, so humanity has passed through these three periods in science. Now, [humanity] has advanced to the point that, having put away what is childish, it sees the idleness and barrenness of all theological and metaphysical speculation. It has now come to the awareness that empiricism and induction are the foundations of all science, that the human mind thus cannot ascend to the unseen and eternal things, nor can it penetrate through to the ground of phenomena. Owing to their metaphysical character, not only God and divine matters but also the essence and attributes [and the] causes and purposes of things are completely unknowable to humanity. Humanity should thus limit itself to the study of sense-perceptible phenomena; and the highest goal it must set for itself is to become acquainted with these phenomena in their mutual connectedness, and to trace the laws that govern their simultaneity and succession. Formerly, science was defined as an investigation into the essence and cause of things, as a *rerum cognoscere causas* [knowing the causes of things]. Now it must be understood as a striving to become acquainted with the relationship of things, as a *rerum cognoscere nexum* [knowing the connection of things]. And whereas humanity once thought it could ascend from the visible to the invisible, from the temporal to the eternal, from the relative to the absolute, and from there once again to view all things *sub specie aeternitatis* [from the standpoint of the eternal], it now universally has only to recognize the relative; *tout est relatif, voilà le seul principe absolu* [everything is relative; that is the only absolute principle].[1]

1. Auguste Comte, *Algemeene Grondslagen der stellige wijsbegeerte* (The Hague: Belinfante, 1846); Émile Littré, *Analyse raisonnée du cours de philosophie positive de M. Auguste Comte* (Utrecht: Kemink, 1845); John Stuart Mill, *Auguste Comte et le positivisme* (Paris: Baillière, 1868), 6; cf. E. L. Fischer, *Die modernen Ersatzversuche für das aufgegebene Christenthum* (Regensburg: Manz, 1903), 29.

Science is certainly losing ground as a result, because all that might lie behind or above the phenomena is unknown land to it. It can express nothing about the matter, either positively or negatively, and is doomed to abstentionism and agnosticism, impotence, and ignorance with regard to unseen things. All of this terrain, if it exists, must be relinquished to subjective opinion. Whoever feels a desire or need to [do so] can populate this unknown land with the postulates of practical reason, with the judgments of his own values, with the creations of his imagination, with the ideals of his heart, with the representations of his religion. There is even room for ghosts, the spirits of the dead, and demonic powers in this airy realm of the unknown. Positivism leaves room for all kinds of so-called compensations for [the loss of] religion, for a cult of humanity, for a veneration of departed spirits, for an altar to the unknown God, even for a worship of Satan. All this, after all, is beyond science and is a private affair; there is something here for everyone.

But according to the positivist view, what science loses in terrain, it gains in inner certainty. For it limits itself to the knowledge of sense-perceptible phenomena; and attempting to trace out its mutual relations, it can finally bring about an understanding of the present from the past and predict the future from the present with indubitable certainty. And that is the ideal of science. Just as astronomy determines the phenomena in the sky far in advance, so does science calculate what will happen as a consequence of the facts it perceives. *Savoir, d'où prévoir; science, d'où prévoyance* [knowledge, from which comes foresight; science comes from foresight].[2] While religion thus remains a "private matter" [*Privatsache*], officially and publicly only the positive is recognized, and only what science says counts. Formerly, state and church proclaimed their authoritative dogmas, but from now on, science, represented by an Areopagus of scholars, must authoritatively determine what should apply in public life. It shall become the "leader of the future" [*Führerin der Zukunft*] and work on the "higher formation of humanity" [*Höherbildung der Menschheit*].[3] Formerly, religion held all the power. But "today it is science that, like the truth of which it is the expression and revelation, is called to world domination. The governance of the world belongs to science rather than to divinity, to science as the benefactor of the people and the liberator of humanity."[4]

This is now the general prevailing concept of science. It is true that people give little or no consideration to the "epistemology" [*Wissenschaftslehre*] to which they are committed. They take it for granted that the concept of

2. Here Bavinck alludes to Comte's concept of science as grounded in foresight (*prévoyance*), albeit without directly citing a particular work.—Eds.

3. Ludwig Stein, *Die sociale Frage im Lichte der Philosophie,* 2nd ed. (Stuttgart: Enke, 1903), 534; Mill, *Auguste Comte et la positivisme*, 101; Adolphe-Charles Clavel, *La morale positive* (Paris: Bailliere, 1873), 53, 78, 203, etc.

4. A. Malvert, *Wissenschaft und Religion* (Frankfurt: Neuer Frankfurter Verlag, 1904), 124. [The quotation is originally in German: "heute ist es die Wissenschaft, die gleich der Wahrheit, deren Ausdruck und Offenbarung sie ist, zur Weltherrschaft berufen ist. Der Wissenschaft gehört von nun an anstatt der Gottheit die Weltregierung, der Wissenschaft als der Wohltäterin der Völker und der Befreierin der Menschheit."—Eds.]

science is fixed and has been elevated above all criticism; and thus they are amazed when someone draws the correctness of this concept into doubt or earnestly disputes them. They are imprisoned in the dogma of the theory of presuppositionless science and hold it to be absolute, though they declare everything else to be relative. Thus also Mr. Levy,[5] who can hardly be described as a friend of positivism, says that absolutely no one is uncertain about the concept of science, *in contrast to faith*.[6] Even though he emphasizes this addition, he nonetheless judges that there can only be talk of nuancing the *definition* of science, but not of uncertainty regarding its *concept*—as though the "nuancing" of the definition is not actually rooted in a different view of its concept.

Recently, an unnamed author[7] in the *Handelsblad*[8] spoke in the same spirit:

> Everything [but also only that which is] related to the unprejudiced [*onbevooroordeelde*] search for the truth is scientific. Certainly, we are not unaware that a human being's proper knowledge is based on preconceptions—pre-preconceptions [*vóór-veronderstellingen*]—which, by virtue of the structure of their

5. Here Bavinck has in mind Isaäc Abraham Levy (1836–1920), a Dutch Jewish advocate and politician. Levy was a noted Kantian. See, for example, Jacob Domela Nieuwenhuis, *Levensbericht van Mr. I. A. Levy* (Baarn: Hollandia, 1916), 33.—Eds.

6. J. A. Levy, *Bijzondere Universiteiten* (The Hague: Belinfante, 1904), 17–18.

7. In the original text, Bavinck refers to "Q.N.," an abbreviation of the Latin *quem novisti* (whom you knew), a commonly used abbreviation in anonymized Dutch newspaper articles in that period.—Eds.

8. The *Algemeen Handelsblad*, the most important liberal Dutch daily newspaper in the nineteenth century.—Eds.

> minds, demarcate the paths for every investigation. Science can never be free from such rules of thought without such prior judgments [*vóór-oordeelen*]. To demand this of science would be preposterous. But there are prior judgments [*vóór-oordeelen*], and there are prejudices [*vooróórdeelen*]. And there can never be too much emphasis on demanding that science keeps itself free from these, from prejudices [*vooróórdeelen*]. The servant of science must be able to remain completely unconcerned about the final destination to which his path winds. The scientific man sets out not knowing where he will end up. . . . Whoever binds himself to a predetermined itinerary when it comes to the final destination of his journey does not serve science, but betrays it.[9]

That is also ultimately the reasoning of Prof. Groenewegen, which boils down to this: science is acquired through normal methodology, well-grounded and rounded, and thus [yields] reliably satisfying knowledge. Certainly, there is no science without assumptions, which either as starting points or working hypotheses first make the study possible. Alongside this, the human mind never works as a purely logical machine and can never escape the influence of its affective and volitional life. Even the most levelheaded thinker cannot and may not free himself

9. "De zoogenaamde vrijmaking van het universitair onderwijs," *Algemeen Handelsblad*, May 11, 1903. ["The so-called liberation of university education."—Eds.]

from what lives in his soul in the way of heart persuasions, deeper insight and understanding, higher conception and intimate conviction. But the scientific man uses his assumptions only as long as they serve him, and maintains his standpoint only as long as it appears tenable. Neutrality in the sense of being detached from and indifferent to his most sacred convictions is either an absurdity or, if it were possible, a sin. But neutrality in the sense of objectivity toward traditional representations and one's own concepts, be it ever so favored, is both a scientific and a religious duty.[10]

10. Herman Groenewegen, "Wetenschap of dogmatisme," *Theologisch tijdschrift* 37 (1903): 399–407.

5

Evaluation of Positivism

When we start to probe the positivist conception of science, we immediately run into all kinds of difficulties. It is quite clear to all that Prof. Groenewegen's description of science as nothing other than a well-grounded and reliable knowledge acquired by a normal method cannot bring us a step further forward. Certainly, there is no one who does not readily agree with this description; the question, however, concerns what the normal method for the acquisition of knowledge actually is, and when knowledge may be deemed well-grounded and reliable. And the distinction that the [aforementioned] anonymous writer makes between permitted prior judgments and unpermitted prejudices is plainly incapable of shedding light on this issue. Once again, there is no one who does not accept this distinction wholeheartedly. The Protestant or Roman Catholic scholar who recognizes the confession of his church as truth on the basis of divine authority maintains that it is precisely through this truth that he is better protected from many errors, and better equipped than others for unbiased research. And this cannot be otherwise; truth liberates. If we assume momentarily that the orthodox [scholar] is right in regarding the Holy Scriptures as God's word, then it is clear that this recognition does not stand in the way of scientific research but rather guides it in the right direction. [In the same way, it is clear] that the rejection of that word [of God] is precisely a prejudice that must have a detrimental effect on scientific research. This is all the more so because no one can deny that men of science constantly make mistakes, are always in conflict with one another, and constantly revise the results of their research. A truth that guides science in its research, and protects it from many errors, should not be set aside. Rather, it should be gratefully accepted.

It is true that the moderns[1] now deny the authority of Scripture and oppose a special revelation of truth. But

1. Here Bavinck alludes to the "modern theologians," a school of thought emanating from the theological faculty of Leiden University in the second half of the nineteenth century and led by the likes of Johannes Scholten (1811–1885) and Abraham Kuenen (1828–1891). As a movement, it was antisupernaturalistic, espoused a strict material determinism, and applied higher critical methods to the study of Scripture as a human text.—Eds.

this should not be the decisive factor in the question that concerns us. If the science that accepts special revelation is to be deemed prejudiced beforehand, then the question is certainly soon decided, but [the one who levels this charge] also becomes guilty of *petitio principii* [begging the question][2] and, a priori, assumes as proved what must be proved. It is the reality of special revelation that is precisely in dispute. If God has communicated knowledge of himself in a special way, then it goes without saying that science must reckon with that, and failing to do so, it is guilty of disobedience and error. In the same way, conversely, to assume a special revelation if such has *not* taken place is not a permissible prior judgment but an impermissible prejudice. However, the acceptance [or denial] of special revelation is a question not of science but of religion, not of the head alone but, in the first place, of the heart. And this is why science may not place itself unilaterally on one side and condemn the other conviction in advance as unscientific. This is made all the more significant by the fact that, among the believers, there are certainly men of science who are partisan in their research; but the same also applies, to no lesser extent, to the unbelievers. There is a hatred against God and religion, against Christ and Scripture, against church and confession, which often clouds the clearest mind and confuses the most lucid thinking. Modernists must also be convinced

2. Bavinck is referring to the logical fallacy of *petitio principii*, in which, either explicitly or implicitly, a premise presumes the conclusion to be demonstrated.—Eds.

of this; they can neither deny nor approve the contempt toward religion that so often reverberates in the work of scientific men. After all, they still believe in the objective truth of religion and thus in the existence and the knowability of God. However, for the positivist and materialist, this faith is qualitatively just as foolish and equally unscientific as accepting any special revelation. Why then do they continually direct their attack toward believers and always take the side of science, when from this side they are just as excluded as orthodoxy? In the struggle against contemporary science, it is in no way only about belief in special revelation but also about objective truth, about the right and value of religion.

This already shows that the antithesis "science or religion" is untenable and in any case is inappropriate in the mouth of a modern theologian. For in the eyes of a consistent positivist, he himself—if in truth, he is a modern theologian and still clings to the truth of religion, and thus to the existence of God—is a dogmatist of the purest kind. Whether someone stands on the side of science or dogmatism depends wholly on the standpoint of the person who sizes him up and judges him. Objectively, to draw a line that applies to all [and shows] where science ends and dogmatism begins is just as impossible theoretically as practically. Dr. Groenewegen himself provides a telling proof of this.[3] He recognizes that even the most

3. Herman Groenewegen, "Wetenschap of dogmatisme," *Theologisch tijdschrift* 37 (1903): 405.

levelheaded thinker cannot and may not free himself from whatever lives in his soul by way of heart conviction, deeper insight and discernment, higher conception and intimate conviction. But he soon adds: it is not an indifferentism toward a religion when a person repeatedly investigates the tenability of the historical, literary, or philosophical concepts to which his life of faith is fastened; but it is indifferentism against the truth when a person always has to better the searching of his religious faith, more than anything else, but he confines himself so tightly to his dogmas that he is left with nothing but an anathema to all knowledge [*weten*], thinking, and believing that is not in accord with them. This last clause is now nothing other than an anathema, pronounced by the liberals upon the heads of those who, in their judgment, straitjacket themselves in dogmas—an accusation that contains nothing less than indifferentism against the truth. And, in fact, the entirety of Dr. Groenewegen's reasoning boils down to this: that in order to be impartial, the man of science must abandon not the modern but rather the orthodox view of religion. And as such, everyone follows his manner of reasoning. No one who thinks things through can deny that the scientific researcher also brings with him all kinds of religious, moral, and philosophical convictions and is ruled by them to a greater or lesser degree. But each party argues that its convictions are good and useful prior judgments and, on the other hand, that those of the other party are harmful and disadvantageous prejudices. The Roman Catholics and the Protestants, the Lutherans and the Reformed, the orthodox and the moderns only pass themselves off as impartial and their opponents as partial and prejudiced. Their practice of history provides compelling demonstration of this. Where things are now, it is presumptuous for one of the parties to present itself as representing "the" science and to push all the others into the corner of dogmatism. After all, the question that divides us runs precisely across the boundary between useful prior judgments and deleterious prejudices.

The boundary, which is theoretically impossible to draw, is also practically impossible to identify. No party has the audacity to claim of the other that it has delivered nothing in the field of science and that it can deliver nothing; no single direction or school shall be so bold as to assert that it provides only pure truth, and its opponent, only error. It is true that for years, the tone taken toward orthodoxy by the acolytes of the modern worldview has been extremely haughty and presumptuous. But gradually a change has come for the better. Many now recognize that the direction formerly advocated was often one-sided, that the nomination of professors left much to be desired in terms of impartiality,[4] that there are also reputable men of science among the orthodox. Now, no

4. In 1889, Bavinck himself was passed over for an appointment as professor at his alma mater, Leiden University, on account of his orthodox presuppositions. See James Eglinton, *Bavinck: A Critical Biography* (Grand Rapids, MI: Baker Academic, 2020), 165–67.—Eds.

modern person who moves with the times and is not too tightly confined to his dogmas can simply write off the studies in philosophy, literature, the natural sciences, and history by men of Roman or Protestant confession. Conversely, Christians have never been so narrow-minded as to reject as lies all the scientific investigations carried out by nonbelievers. From the first centuries onward, they highly valued classical philosophy and literature. They inspected and sifted through them, and took over the good with gratefulness and profited from it. And in the present day, who would consider the effort and sacrifice devoted to the service of science by unbelievers as small, and reject the brilliant results obtained by their diligent work and tireless perseverance? Without exception, all enjoy the enrichment and increased pleasantness of life that has been obtained in this day and age through ingenious inventions and surprising discoveries. In no way does the Christian have a right or reason to look down with contempt on the investigations and outcomes of science. After all, [Christians] believe that God, the same God that they profess in Christ to be their Father, makes the sun rise over the evil and the good, and reigns over the just and the unjust. Every good and perfect gift comes down from the Father of lights, with whom there is no variation or shadow of change. If they nonetheless make themselves guilty by disregarding these gifts, they would be not only unjust against men but also ungrateful toward God.

Religion and science, faith and knowledge [*geloof en kennis*], purity of heart and clarity of head, and likewise sin and falsehood, unrighteousness and heresy, immoral life and ungodly doctrine are indubitably connected with one another. That connection is often much closer than we suspect or dare to express. François Coppée[5] once acknowledged that he was dissuaded from the Christian faith of his upbringing due to the shortcomings of his youth and the shame of confessing wrongdoing. And many, he says, who are in the same situation as he, if they were willing to be honest, would have to admit that what alienated them from the faith in the first place was only the strict law that religion imposed on their sensuality, and that only in later years did they feel the need to condone and justify the violations of the moral law by way of a scientific system.[6] But no matter how close the connection may be, they [religion and science, etc.] are not identical. The person who believes in Christ is not automatically a scientific person; and the person who does not believe is not automatically a liar or a lunatic. In terms of natural gifts, believers can lag far behind non-believers—the children of this world are more prudent in dealing with their own generation than children of

5. François Coppée (1842–1908), a French poet and novelist, and member of the *Académie Française*. Having abandoned the Roman Catholicism of his youth, Coppée reembraced Catholicism following a serious illness in 1898, and published the novel *La bonne souffrance* (Paris: Lemerre, 1898) as a reflection on this experience.—Eds.

6. Victor Cathrein, *Glauben und Wissen: Eine Orientierung in den religiösen Grundproblemen der Gegenwart für alle Gebildeten* (Freiburg: Herder, 1903), 172.

the light. A repellent and scornful dogmatism can arise among Christians, just as a capacious, beneficial vision can arise among non-Christians.

But all this proves nothing with regard to the truth of the positivist conception of science. The first thing that the advocates of this view have to learn is that their definition of science is just one alongside others. Of course, each party presents its opinion as the true one, and it must do so, for otherwise it would acknowledge simultaneously that it does not mean what it says. But with this, we too must always remember that our view is not the only one in the world, and that, in addition to ours, there are others that have equal rights in the practice of life. If we do not recognize this, we become intolerant and exclusive, and we are not far from striving to suppress all others with violence. But this is precisely what is against the nature of science and the character of truth. These will not, and may not, rule by force or coercion, by state power or ecclesial rule, but solely and only through ethical means, through their inner power, through the strength of their argumentation. Mr. Levy accused Dr. Kuyper of being the minister of ecclesial absolutism, having learned from Thomas Hobbes,[7] the representative of worldly absolutism.[8] But that accusation only demonstrates that Mr. Levy is so entrenched in his own dogma

7. Thomas Hobbes (1588–1679), the English political philosopher and author of the influential work *Leviathan*.—Eds.

8. J. A. Levy, *Bijzondere Universiteiten* (The Hague: Belinfante, 1904), 8.

that he does not understand the principles and objectives of his opponents. After all, the struggle for the liberation of higher education is precisely against the monopoly of scientific knowledge from a single direction, and has no other goal than to ensure that the various directions in science can freely wrestle with one another in society, and that competition is not rendered impossible through the granting of state privileges to one but not the other.

In itself, of course, it is quite conceivable that the state, too, has a certain confession and maintains it in all public institutions. But liberalism itself opposed this, made the state neutral, and declared all churches, confessions, and outlooks equal in rights. If, therefore, there is a considerable group within the nation who demand freedom and equality on the basis of the declaration of rights for the church, school, or the university, liberalism must support it because of its own *principle*, but it opposes it just as regularly in practice. That is the antinomy that [liberalism] repeatedly places before itself, and that makes clear to all that it is very liberal in word but highly illiberal in deed. The principle seems to be afraid of its own application. That is demonstrated in the primary school struggle, and it has come to the fore again in the issue of higher education.[9] It is precisely the so-called "presupposition-

9. Here Bavinck refers to the struggle for equal state funding for specifically Christian primary schools, and for private (*bijzondere*) Christian universities, as compared with funding given by the state to "neutral" primary schools and state universities. This struggle eventually ended in 1917, when the Dutch government agreed to support all schools equally.—Eds.

less" [*voraussetzungslose*] science, which outlaws any other view, that claims sole dominion for itself and places state power and state funds in its own service. Therefore, before all things, this should be taught: that the positivist concept of science is one view among others. Of course, it cannot simply give up the pretention that it is the true view, but it must refrain from using anything other than ethical means to establish this conviction. It must tolerate [the fact] that others do not agree with it and present a wholly different view of science. For it is not only later, during the practice, method, and result of science, that the difference in world-and-life view, in religious and ethical convictions, has an influence, but right from the start, during the definition of the concept of science. The concept of science is not obtained from observation and experience; it is not a result of empirical research, but it is a philosophical concept that is handed to us in our thinking, in connection with the whole of our worldview.

6

Consequence of the Verdict

The concept of "presuppositionless" [*voraussetzungslose*] science is evidently a fruit of positivist philosophy. This philosophy is just as good, and to the same degree systematic, a philosophy as the philosophy of Plato and Aristotle, of Schelling and Hegel. And it is not *the* [only] philosophy [worthy of the term], but the philosophical worldview of a specific thinker and of a relatively small group of people who follow him. It first appeared around the middle of the last century, then flourished for a short time and would have already gone bankrupt in scientific circles were it not introduced recently by Richard Avenarius[1] under a

1. Richard Avenarius (1843–1896), a German-Swiss philosopher who argued for a radical form of positivism known as empirio-criticism.—Eds.

different name and in a different form and thus accepted again by some. This empirical criticism also emerged with the claim that it is the only truly scientific [approach], is based exclusively on facts of experience, and denies the transcendence of all existence. But this direction, too, has had to hear the reproach of none less than Wundt,[2] [who argued] that it does not accept experience without prejudices but, rather, views it in light of a particular metaphysic and is guilty of scholasticism in its conceptual constructions.[3] It was even pointed out from various sides, and not without reason, that it makes everything subjective, sees only psychological phenomena in logic, ethics, religion, and so on, and thus leads to skepticism, to the destruction of all knowledge of the truth.[4]

It is not difficult, then, to perceive that positivism is a specific philosophy and, like any other, proceeds on the basis of certain metaphysical assumptions. It is not even possible to provide an epistemology [*Erkenntnistheorie*] without metaphysics and philosophy; whoever proclaims a particular thesis about it embraces some system of philosophy, whether consciously or unconsciously. In his *Levensbeschouwing*, Allard Pierson[5] is therefore

2. Wilhelm Wundt (1832–1920), a German scholar known as the father of experimental psychology.—Eds.

3. Constantin Gutberlet, *Der Kampf um die Seele: Vorträge über die brennenden Fragen der modernen Psychologie*, vol. 1 (Mainz: Kirchheim, 1903), 6.

4. Georg Wobbermin, *Theologie und Metaphysik: Das Verhältnis der Theologie zur modernen Erkenntnistheorie und Psychologie* (Berlin: Duncker 1901), 82ff.

5. Allard Pierson (1831–1896), a Dutch liberal theologian who later gained prominence as an art historian. For a historical analysis of Pierson in relation to neo-Calvinism, see Arie L. Molendijk, *Protestant Theology and Modernity in Nineteenth-Century Netherlands* (Oxford: Oxford University Press, 2022), chap. 3.—Eds.

quite right in speaking of philosophical ground-principles when he deals with the origin, nature, and boundaries of our knowledge.[6] And the first philosophical principle [*grondbeginsel*], then, is this: that our knowledge flows out of nothing other than sense perception and experience. This is indeed a philosophical thesis [*grondstelling*], and not one that is self-evident or as clear as day. Rather, it contains within itself a whole worldview and is only counted as truth by a relatively small circle of people. According to its history and scientific research, the rest of humanity has had a different idea. [In that light], the opinion that on this hypothesis, we stand on a firm foundation of visible and indubitable reality is naive as a result of its superficiality.

Here we merely point out that all scientific research assumes in advance and without proof the reliability of the senses and the objectivity of the perceivable world. These things are not provable. Those who doubt them cannot be refuted by any arguments. Skepticism is more an issue of the heart than of the head. The reality of the world outside us is fixed by and for faith. To accept it is an act of trust; most profoundly [it is an act] of trust in the truthfulness of God.[7] After all, the outside world is only given to us in our psychical representations. We are not able to compare these with the outside world itself

6. Allard Pierson, *Eene levensbeschouwing* (Haarlem: Kruseman & Tjeenk Willink, 1875), 65.

7. René Descartes, *Principia philosophiae*, 2.1; J. P. N. Land, *Inleiding tot de wijsbegeerte* (The Hague: Nijhoff, 1900), 97.

and cannot withdraw from ourselves. We must simply believe that in these representations a real knowledge of the world is offered to us. If we do not want that, there is nothing left but the psychologism currently held by many, which, according to Münsterberg,[8] is the last phase of naturalism and regards true and false judgments in the same way, [seeing both simply] as the results of the course of representations.[9]

But even if we dispense with this, sense perception itself is not as simple as it appears to many. As Pierson rightly says, there is no such thing as a pure observer. In the first place, there is no perceiver [and thus no perception], or there must be a person who perceives, and what and how he perceives depends on his circumstances. Indeed, it is not the eye or the ear that perceives but the person who sees through the eye and hears through the ear. Perception is a psychical activity—not a passive state but a positive action by which the subject makes its influence felt. The observation of facts always depends on subjectivity. There is [also] a willful blindness. The influence of subjectivity is much stronger still when perceptions are connected. In fact, all perception is already a joining of sensations. All our words are names of objects that are not susceptible to perception. We do not perceive a dog or a chair but combine various perceptions into a single representation, which we express in the name *dog*

8. Hugo Münsterberg (1863–1916), a German-American psychologist.—Eds.
9. Gutberlet, *Der Kampf um die Seele*, 1:48.

or *chair*, and at the same time we add the thing perceived to a class of known objects with which it bears a certain resemblance.[10]

In other words, no perception—in the actual, scientific sense—can happen without thinking. In scientific investigation, this activity is threefold. First, it sends sense perception in a particular direction, picks out a particular group of phenomena, and isolates these from the totality of the world [*wereldgeheel*], and abstracts and combines the perceived phenomena. Moreover, thinking immediately brings all kinds of starting points and assumptions to scientific work. Aristotle already perceived that there is and must be not only a mediate but also an immediate knowledge [*weten*]. Although he rejected Plato's doctrine of ideas and derived all knowledge [*kennis*] from experience, he nonetheless understood that all proofs must ultimately rest on a self-evident, unprovable truth. The proofs must, of course, be retraceable to such propositions, which are themselves immediately certain.[11] All science therefore proceeds from such so-called axioms. Finally, the activity of thinking consists in the effort to trace the connection, the idea, the law, in the phenomena, in order to arrive at true science.[12] It thus proceeds

10. Pierson, *Eene levenbeschouwing*, 66.

11. Eduard Zeller, *Die Philosophie der Griechen in ihrer geschichtlichen Entwicklung*. vol. 3 (Leipzig: Fues's Verlag [R. Reisland], 1880), 195, 235, 236; Cornelius Spruyt, *Proeve van eene geschiedenis van de leer der aangeboren begrippen* (Leiden: Brill, 1879), 33.

12. "Science only begins when spirit seizes control of matter, when an attempt is made to subject the mass of experience to a rational cognition; it is the spirit turned toward matter." Alexander von Humboldt, *Kosmos: Entwurf*

from the tacit but significant assumption that in the phenomena there resides unity, order, thought, logos—a logos that corresponds with the logos in the human mind [*geest*]. In full confidence it thus applies the laws of thinking, and not only these alone but all kinds of metaphysical concepts, such as thing, property, cause, effect, law, condition, time, space, truth, falsehood, and more, to the perceived phenomena. Scientific research cannot rid itself of these. And with this, it also demonstrates that it cannot do without philosophy and metaphysics.

Positivism thus already appears to be untenable on the terrain of sense perception. It is even more strongly refuted, however, by the phenomena of internal experience. The independence and particularity of these phenomena is denied by Comte, Avenarius, and many of the newer psychologists, who also dispute internal experience as a specific source of knowledge alongside sense perception. Indeed, it cannot be denied that we are only gradually becoming aware of the distinction between the phenomena of external and internal perception, and that the phenomena of external perception are also only directly given to us through the consciousness. But by contrast to this, the distinction between the two groups of phenomena necessarily comes to the fore in our consciousness as soon as

---

einer physischen Weltbeschreibung, vol. 1 (Stuttgart: Cotta, 1844), 67, 69, in Martin von Nathusius, *Das Wesen der Wissenschaft und ihre Anwendung auf die Religion: Empirische Grundlegung für die theologische Methodologie* (Leipzig: Hinrichs, 1885), 67. [German original: "Wissenschaft fängt erst an, wo der Geist sich des Stoffes bemächtigt, wo versucht wird, die Masse der Erfahrungen einer Vernunfterkenntniss zu unterwerfen; sie ist der Geist, zugewandt zu der Natur."]

we try to observe and think about them somewhat intentionally. There is certainly a great difference between the representations as they—although immanent with us—refer, by their very nature, to things outside us and the same representations, being, as they are, activities and revelations of our own psychical life. And alongside this are all those representations [*voorstellingen*], affections [*aandoeningen*], and decisions of the will. Although these do not emerge without influence from the outside world, they nonetheless indicate states within ourselves, rather than outside ourselves.[13]

With these facts regarding our consciousness in view, the distinction between the physical and the psychical, between object and subject, between matter and spirit cannot be rejected. Of course this does not deny that they exist in close connection, and that the conscious life within us comes about through the mediation of physical organs and functions. But even if that connection is much more intimate than what physiological psychology has made us recognize thus far, that would in no way erase the distinction between the two. We know, after all, not only of visible but also of invisible things; we are conscious of sensations, representations, affections, decisions of the will, which cannot be perceived with the senses and yet possess an undeniable reality. In the life of the soul [*zieleleven*] we have to do with facts that are more fixed

13. Wobbermin, *Theologie und Metaphysic*, 89.

in our awareness, indeed, that stand firmer than the sensible phenomena. [In the life of the soul] powers present themselves before our consciousness that are far stronger than physical compulsion. Affections [*aandoeningen*], passions [*hartstochten*], convictions, decisions of the will, and so on are realities just as much as matter and force, even though they cannot be seen with the eyes or felt by the hands. And if this is so, the thesis that only the sense-perceptible exists, and that this alone constitutes the object and content of our science, is untenable.

Besides, many have modified positivism on this point, recognizing psychical reality alongside physical reality and, in connection with this, adopting internal experience alongside external experience as an organ of knowledge [*kennis*]. And yet, they maintain that on the terrain of mental [*geestelijke*] phenomena, only the empirical method may be applied, and that there may not be any a priori assumptions, no faith in any sense whatsoever. Of course, all those objections which were already briefly raised against the empirical method as applied to physical phenomena then return in all their power. Here, too, one must proceed from the reliability of the organs of perception and the laws of thought; to accept the reality of that psychical world is an unproven assumption; and the hypothesis that there [in that psychical world], order and rule, thought and law reign is a great [exercise of] faith that can only rest, ultimately, in the truthfulness of God.

But this is [noted only] in passing. Another objection is that compared with the study of this, on this terrain, the empirical, deductive method can be applied purely even much less on the terrain [of the inner life]. Indeed, the life of the soul is so immeasurably rich and so complicated that it can never as such be made the subject of scientific research. If we were ever to talk of a strictly scientific study of psychical phenomena, then these must each first be disentangled, to some extent, and each viewed in isolation. Research must begin, as it were, by detaching the phenomenon in focus from the context in which it occurs in reality. It must begin by abstracting, and this abstraction is an activity of thought. In advance, [this activity] takes perception into its service, guiding and directing it. What is more, the life of the soul is so broad and so deep that [its] observation [of phenomena] would never stop if thinking did not shed its light on the multitude of phenomena and bring order to the chaos. The empirical method is thus necessary and good, but it is led by the synthetic method from beginning to end.

The main objection, arises, however, through the question of what one has in view in the research of these psychical phenomena. If [the goal is] only knowledge [*kennis*] of the psychological process—the existence, connection, distinction, and development of representations [*voorstellingen*] in the individual, in a nation, in humanity—we cannot go beyond psychology and let all of the humanities [*geesteswetenschappen*] be taken up into psychology. But that has never been the conception and purpose of these sciences. It has always been their endeavor to arrive at objective reality from the representations [*voorstellingen*] of the subject. That was and is still generally true of those representations within us that refer to a physical world outside us. People do not want only to consider the psychological process of these representations. Rather, through and from these representations, [they also want] to become acquainted with the material world. The same applies to those representations that do not refer to a sensory nature of that sort. They too refer to a reality, but of a spiritual [*geestelijken*] rather than sensory nature. In our consciousness, we find impressions [*beseffen*], perceptions [*gewaarwoordingen*], representations [*voorstellingen*], and so on that point to a realm of the true, good, and beautiful. We can, of course, investigate and study these impressions [*beseffen*], and the like, from their psychological side, but then we receive merely knowledge of an empirical reality that has its basis only in the subject. Natural science and history do not have to do—at least, not ultimately at least—with the knowledge [*kennis*] of the development of human representations but [deal] with the knowledge [*kennis*] of nature and history itself. Likewise the intended goal of our study of psychical representations in the narrow sense is not the knowledge [*kennis*] of the process of these representations [*voorstellingen*] but the knowledge [*kennis*] of the mental[14] world, of which these human representations [*voorstellingen*] are always an impure imprint [*afdruk*]. All of those who now hold this view of the humanities [*geesteswetenschappen*] have abandoned the foundation of empiricism and positivism and ascended to the world of ideas. There they tread the heights of ontology and metaphysics.

It is true that many do not give thought to their course of action. They constantly speak of the empirical, deductive method as the only true one, and yet at every moment—consciously or unconsciously—apply the synthetic, deductive method. But that does not take away [the fact] that the results obtained so far are in direct conflict with the positivistic and empirical concept of science. It is not acceptable to say beforehand that a person sets to work in scientific research without prejudice and proceeds from nothing but sensible or internally observable facts and phenomena, and yet from the outset continually brings along all sorts of assumptions that are not the fruit of empiricism but rather have a philosophical and metaphysical character. Above all, it is not acceptable to see unbiased observation as the only source of knowledge [*kennis*] while also recognizing all kinds of norms in the fields of logic, ethics, religion, and aesthetics, which claim to possess absolute authority. Either there is only empirical, historical reality, but then there is no religion other

14. The term used by Bavinck here, *geestelijke wereld*, is ambiguous and could be translated as "spiritual world" or "mental world."—Eds.

than as a psychological phenomenon, and alongside this, there are also no logic and no ethics, no truth and no virtue, no beauty and no right; following this, true and false judgments both have an equal right to exist; both are necessary—they are products of the process of development of our representations, just as good and evil courses of action are the necessary consequences of inborn and acquired tendencies. Or there are absolute norms, and there is a realm of ideas above empirical reality—a realm of the true, good, and beautiful; however, if that is so, the positivist and empirical concept of science cannot be maintained.

In part, the proponents of this view of science have themselves recognized this, insofar as they have limited the field of science and surrounded it with an "unknown land." Pulling back from materialism, positivism has sought its redemption in abstention and the confession of not knowing [*niet-weten*]. But in doing so, it has not left the matter at hand in a better condition. For not only does it remain on the terrain to which it has confined itself, where it is subject to all of the above objections, but it also entangles itself in an inner contradiction. The statement that all that is metaphysical and ontological is unknowable nevertheless contains a science replete with content. To assert the unknowability [of all that is metaphysical and ontological], one must have a clear understanding of it. Whoever says that God, the true, the good, and the beautiful cannot be known also pronounces that he believes in their existence and that he has some knowledge of them, namely, as much knowledge as is needed to maintain on solid ground that he does not know them. When properly considered, agnosticism is thus at odds with itself. Either its proponents are tied to a very particular concept of God, or it contains the denial of all that is absolute and is thus merely a different, less offensive name for materialism and atheism.

Finally, therefore, attention must be drawn to two very distinct things that positivism constantly confuses with one another. If [positivism] says, *tout est relatif, voilà le seul principe absolu* [the only absolute is that everything is relative],[15] then it is indeed true that all our knowledge [*kennis*], of both the visible and the invisible, is relative, finite, and imperfect. All our knowledge [*weten*] is fragmentary and unfinished. We know [*kennen*] in part. But this recognition is something completely different from Comte's hypothesis that everything is relative. [This is so] because there is a great distinction between the properties of our knowing [*kennen*] and the properties of the object of our knowledge [*kennis*]. No conclusion can be drawn from the former to the latter. There is no contradiction at all in the idea that the absolute exists and that we possess only a very relative knowledge [*kennis*] of it. The relative does not become absolute because we might eventually

15. Here Bavinck cites Auguste Comte's famous formula.—Eds.

know [*kennen*] it absolutely and fully, and the absolute does not become relative because we know [*kennen*] it merely in a relative, limited, and defective sense.[16] As long as one does not mean to deny the existence of the absolute, one cannot put too much emphasis on the relativity of our knowledge. What we really know is minor in content and small in scope. Kant and Comte have made us deeply aware of this. They have failed, as scholastics sometimes have, in that they have tried to draw a sharp geometric line between what could be precisely known and what could be believed on subjective grounds. There is no such boundary to which we can point. The world does not allow itself to be divided into two halves; neither can the human being be divided into two persons. "If we do away with everything that is in fact only a scientific belief to us, science shrinks to a small remainder of sentences whose content is so dull and insignificant that it is hardly worth the effort of investigation."[17] There is no point at which to indicate where believing [*geloven*] ends and knowing [*weten*] begins. The inductive method is always led by the deductive. All science lies on the foundation of metaphysical assumptions. Objectively, the cause of this is that the

16. E. L. Fischer, *Die modernen Ersatzversuche für das aufgegebene Christenthum* (Regensburg: Manz, 1903), 63.

17. Hermann Ulrici, *Gott und die Natur*, 2nd ed. (Leipzig: Weigel, 1866), 9. [German original: "Streichen wir alles hinweg, was uns in Wahrheit nur ein wissenschaftlicher Glaube ist, so schrumpft die Wissenschaft zusammen zu einem kleinen Rest von Sätzen, deren Inhalt so dürftig und unbedeutend ist, dass er die Mühe der Forschung kaum lohnt."]

invisible things are revealed in the visible, and the visible leads to the invisible. We even have some knowledge of God, who is the origin of all things. Upon further investigation, the very least that we know of his works itself contains an unfathomable mystery.

7

The Concept of Science

To obtain a clear view into the essence and goal of science, we cannot do better than proceed from normal empirical knowing. After all, being precedes thinking. Humanity lived for epochs before the functions of that life were narrowly researched in physiology. [Humanity] thought before the laws of thinking were set out in logic. [Humanity] spoke and gifted existence to languages before anyone occupied himself with the study of grammar. [Humanity] was a realm that shared in religious, moral, legal, and civil life before a single scientific theory about these had seen the light of day. [Humanity] brought agriculture and industry, profession and business to a high state of development before science worried about its existence. Everywhere, life precedes philosophy. Scientific knowing [*wetenschappelijke weten*] may perhaps be the most noble fruit of the human spirit [*geest*], [but] it is certainly not the root from which life springs up. Culture does indeed contain within it a certain degree of knowledge: religion, morality, justice, beauty, state, society, industry, agriculture, and so on presuppose the consciousness of the human being; they are all built on senses, representations, and thoughts. But the knowledge that lies in these is of an empirical nature. It is the fruit of attentive perception and practical experience, is related to wisdom, and as such, is obtainable for everyone.

Nonetheless this empirical knowing [*weten*] is of the highest significance; it is the condition and foundation of the entire human life. There is no justification for looking down on it from on high. Whoever takes a skeptical stance against it beforehand, and first expects certainty from science, undermines the foundation upon which all science rests. In this empirical knowing, the human being does not limit his knowledge to the things that are perceptible by the senses, but rather expands it to those things that are invisible and spiritual. In everyday life, we know [*weten*] not only that the sun rises in the east and goes down in the west, that the seasons change in order, and so on, but we know [*weten*] just as much of the essential distinction between true and untrue, between good and evil, between justice and injustice; we know [*weten*] that stealing is a sin, that evil is punished, that it is illegitimate to do something against the conscience, and so on. Without hesitation, the concept of knowing [*het weten*] is also applied to religious and moral convictions; the Christian knows [*weet*] that his Redeemer lives, that he has gone over from death to life, that he will inherit salvation, and so on.

And yet, in everyday life we are also conscious that the grounds upon which knowing [*weten*] rests vary, and that there are thus degrees of certainty in knowledge. The difference between assuming [*menen*], believing [*geloven*], and knowing [*weten*] is universally recognized. To assume is to take something to be true on the basis of things that the subjective self is convinced are insufficient; it is a [a form of] knowing [*kennen*] that is not objectively evident and that subjectively is not certain. To the contrary, knowing [*weten*] is a knowledge [*kennen*] that is objectively evident and subjectively certain; knowing [*weten*] rests on grounds that are regarded as valid by everyone (perception, proving), and brings with it a certainty that excludes all doubt. Believing is distinguished from both of these. In general, believing is taking [something] to be true on grounds that are sufficient for a defined subject in the given circumstances, and that make doubt appear unreasonable. It yields a knowledge that is not objectively evident for all but is still subjectively certain. Believing stands beneath knowing [*weten*] not in subjective assurance but in objective obviousness; if I know [*weet*] something, I do not have to believe it any more. Everyone feels this when he considers the meaning of sentences like this: "I do believe that it is so"; "I believe that it is going to rain"; "I believe that Mr. N. is an honest man"; and so on. The thought, then, is always [this]: I take it to be true, but I do not know it certainly. In the same sense, believing can occupy itself with religious, moral propositions; if two people reason together on the proofs for God's existence, on the immortality of the soul, on the divinity of Christ, and one of them finally ends by saying, "All things considered, I do still believe that God exists, that the soul is immortal, that Christ is truly God," this believing is nothing else than, and nothing more than, a taking to be true on grounds that are subjectively adequate.

This believing has a broad significance in and for life, because most of what we know [*weten*], by far, we do not acquire by our own perception, research, or reasoning, but through believing, through a taking as true on adequate subjective grounds. There is nothing wrong with this per se. The content of what we know [*weten*] by faith can, in itself, be just as true as what we acquire as knowledge through our own perception and investigation. Everything depends on the character of the grounds on which the believing rests. One of the most important grounds in believing is the witness of another. We believe what we ourselves could not perceive but what we hear from reliable people; in an actual sense, all that falls beyond our own field of vision in the past, present, and future can become the content of my knowledge only through the witness of others who know [*weten*] something about it and who share their science. To the extent that such people are more reliable, the truth of their witness is elevated beyond reasonable doubt and thus enriches my knowledge. One's own perception and another's witness, reason, and authority are two sources from which knowledge flows to us in this life. *Per visionem et fidem ad intellectum* [through vision and faith to the intellect].[1]

However, humanity does not ultimately declare itself satisfied with this empirical knowledge [*kennis*], which humanity has slowly acquired through perception, experience, and survival, and which constitutes the cornerstone of all domestic and civil, political and social, religious and moral life. When a certain level of civilization has been reached, when circumstances arise through which

1. In the field of religion there is an important change in the significance of believing. Everyone feels that when he compares these two expressions: "All things having been considered, I still believe that God exists, that he is almighty, that he created the world"; and "I believe in God, the Father, the Almighty, the Creator of heaven and earth." The first case concerns historical belief, which considers the existence of God and God's act of creation as scientific propositions and, having considered the grounds for and against them, deems them to be acceptable. In the second case, "saving" faith speaks out its confession. In essence, this believing is not a taking [of something] to be true on the basis of intellectual reasonings, and also not a holding of some claim or pronouncement to be true, but rather [it is] a giving over of the soul, in its entirety, to God, who has revealed himself in such a way, a joining [of oneself] to his person, a trusting in his word as *his* word, an embracing of his promise, a confessing that because of his Son Christ, God is *my* God and *my* Father. This faith is of no lower degree than knowing [*weten*], but it is something different from knowing [*weten*]; it is a personal knowing [*kennen*] of God as *my* God [seen] in the face of Christ, in the way, and through the means of his revelation, as *his* revelation.

one no longer has to toil for one's daily bread, when the senses are exercised enough and observation and interest are awakened to a sufficient degree, then gradually an interest emerges in the human being to give an account of the phenomena that present themselves to him. He is not satisfied with the empirical, often superficial and inadequate, knowledge [*kennis*] but rather focuses himself on investigating things methodically and according to plan; he becomes interested not only in knowing [*weten*] *that* there is something but also *why* it is, and is in such a *way*; he pursues the phenomena, disregarding the practical use that could flow forth for [his] life, solely and only to know [*kennen*] them, to look into them in their cause and goal, in their essence and connectedness. As soon as the human being rises to this and finds knowing [*weten*] itself to be a good, as soon as he is no longer satisfied with reality but learns to value the truth as a treasure, the pursuit of which no exertion is too great and no sacrifice too heavy, [it is then that] science in the actual sense is born.

This concept of science is always taken in a twofold sense: that of scientific research and that of scientific result. An area of study is in no sense first called a science only when the ideal, the knowledge of truth, is reached within it; because there is no science that merits that name, understood as such. Virtually all areas of research and teaching move, for the most part, in the stadium of empirical knowing [*weten*]; we know [*kennen*] the facts and phenomena within certain boundaries but do not penetrate their essence, their cause, their laws. Absolutely, this not only is the case in theology and philosophy, in literature and in history but also applies to physics and medical science. Actual medicine is as yet all but entirely grounded on empirical [investigation], and in the present day, physics and chemistry have advanced to the point that they recognize they stand before a world of mysteries. Almost none of us assume that we have found a law in nature or history, in religion or morality, in economics or sociology—or [if we do], we are once again brought to doubt by the discovery of new phenomena. Therefore, under "science" we understand, in most cases, no more than scientific investigation, whether that is considered on the side of the subject, who conducts the investigation, or on the side of the object, which is investigated.

What now belongs under the rubric of scientific research and, as such, has a right to the name *science* is not decided by us a priori, but is rather provided in the passage of history [*historie*] and produced by its events [*geschiedenis*]. Slowly, investigation, the remit of science, the extent of the university, stretches out. Scientific thinking began in Greece with the question of the final ground of things, and from there, all the problems that present themselves to the human mind [*geest*] were developed in good order. The universities were not set up artificially in the Middle Ages, according to a previously established schema but, rather, were first planted as a small sprig, from which they grew like a living organism.

In the present day, the technical subjects are gradually elevating themselves to the highest point of the university's sciences, and these are constantly subject to a powerful evolution. In one word, there has been a development of science in the events of history [*geschiedenis*] that does not happen outside of human thinking and willing, but that also cannot be explained from these, and that points back to a driving idea, to an organized thought. First, when that development has advanced part of the way, it becomes an object of scientific thinking; the human being seeks to know [*kennen*] the idea that animates and dominates the entire development.

From these considerations, the great distinction between empirical and scientific knowing is revealed. Empirical knowing [*weten*] knows [*kent*] the particular, independent phenomena, but scientific knowing [*weten*] seeks the universal, the law, that masters them all, the idea that animates them all. Empirical knowing remains standing before the *that*; scientific knowing moves beyond things to the *why*. Empirical knowing stands in service of the practical consequence and finds its goal in the demands of life; scientific knowing strives for [something] far above this and aims at the knowledge of the truth. There is just as great a distinction between [them] as between the farmer who works his land in the same way as his forefathers and the agriculturalist, who has studied the land and production; as between someone who is a judge of character and the psychologist; as between the practical counselor and the lawyer; as between the religious person and the theologian.

But because of this distinction, important as it may be, the connection and relatedness [between them] should not be overlooked. It should be said that science—also in its highest development—remains bound to life. We can hold science in such high regard [while remembering that] those who practice it remain normal people who cannot live on nothing. There would be far fewer capable men of science if, in many cases, practicing it did not lead to an honorable position and a [financially] independent existence. This is absolutely not to say that all scientific research is only study to make ends meet. The reception of a professorship and the enjoyment of an adequate income can go along with the practice of science from sincere love [for the subject]; it is even so that a carefree life is usually essential for this, just as overabundant luxury is damaging to [the same]. A good worker accomplishes the daily work to which he is obliged in order to maintain his livelihood with desire and with joy; the work itself becomes a pleasure to him. A work of art often owes its existence to an open-minded commission. The motto "science for science's sake" leads to just as great a one-sidedness as that of "art for art's sake."

More significant is that the man of science remains a human being, not only matter, so that he would continue to care about food and drink, about a roof [over his head] and clothing, just like all other people, but [he also remains a human being] in a moral and religious sense. A chemist, who knows the nutrient components of food, is not fed by that knowledge but, rather, like the most ordinary person, is fed only by eating that food. And as such, the man of science can remain living religiously and morally only when he takes unto himself the same food that quiets the spiritual hunger of the poorest day laborer. In this regard there is no difference between the most learned researcher and the simplest citizen. Both have one and the same human nature in common. The same impure, cunning heart abides in both, the same corrupted will, the same straying intellect, the same sinful desire. And both also have the same religious needs, are bound to the same moral law, and are going to meet the same judgment. Whoever perceives this can recognize that science [offers] a lot, but not that it is everything [or] that it is the only thing in human life. Alongside it, religion, morality, [and] art retain their independent place; science will never be qualified to replace or compensate for these, not only for the people but also for those who devote themselves to sciences.

The sources from which scientific knowing draws its knowledge are also the same as those from which empirical knowing flows. If the man of science remains a human being in the full sense, then it is obvious that science cannot strive against religion, against morality, against art—in one word, against life. Perhaps it will be satisfied to explain life, to purify, to lead; but it can never bring forth and may never destroy [life]. Agriculture, livestock breeding, business, [and] industry have much for which to thank science; but they emerged from and existed before [it] through factors that are present in the world and that were not produced by science. Precisely the same is true of religion and morality, of justice and authority, of beauty and art. These exist from and of themselves, are subject to their own laws, and have each their own goal. And science has as its task to recognize this full and rich life, to proceed from it, and to understand it in its essence and truth.

Naturally, this is not to say that science must carry over the content of empirical knowing silently and without critique. Practical knowledge, acquired through perception and experience is not always infallible; it is just as lacking as the popular wisdom laid down in proverbs. Empirical knowing regarding nature and the cosmos, agriculture and livestock breeding, religion and morality, justice and art must always be purified and clarified through science. The farmer acts foolishly when he swears by the old and wants to know [*weten*] nothing of change and improvement. But equally one-sided is the man of science who treats practical experience as worthless and builds up theories in abstraction from life. The lawyer who does not take into account the people's sense of justice makes himself unsuitable to legislate and pass judgment. The medical doctor who looks down on practical experience forgets that his medicine rests on nothing but experience.

And the theologian who considers the religious ideas and affectations of the pious to be worthless undermines the foundation of his own science.

This arrogant scientific posture toward life thus does not work, because it lacks, and [indeed] cannot have, a single source of knowledge that is open to anything other than empirical knowledge. It is true that the scientific man investigates these sources more intentionally and thus also with greater precision than the normal person, but this changes nothing of the fact that both see the same world and perceive it with the same senses. The thinkers and philosophers often considered this to be below them and elevated themselves far above the *vulgus profanum* [common masses]. The aristocracy of many artists who viewed themselves as gods and, as *Uebermenschen* [upper men], looked down on the *Herdentiere* [herd animals] is also not unknown among the men of science.[2] Sometimes they alleged themselves to possess a different organ of perception and to see a different world than the ordinary person. While the masses had to content themselves with sensory perception, with faith, with the appearance of things, [scientists] had speculative reason and contemplation at their disposal, and exalted themselves to the heights of *gnosis* [secret knowledge], where they beheld the mysteries of the invisible world [as though] face to

2. Bavinck is referring to a series of ideas closely linked to Nietzsche, whose philosophy set up the individualistic, dominant "upper man" (*Übermensch*) over the herd-like mass of unthinking, ordinary (and weak) people.—Eds.

face. And when this contemplation seemed not to be accessible in a normal way, an artificial method of asceticism was sometimes conceived in order to participate in the ecstasy. But for science, just as for religion and art, this was always a dangerous experiment that ended up in a cruel and sobering [realization] and deep disappointment.

However high scientific knowledge might elevate itself and however far it might extend itself, it never gets to see a world other than the one that stretches out before every eye, and it never possesses a different organ of perception than the one that every human being has by nature. Nothing can be investigated or discovered by us except things that make up a component part of this world that offers itself to us in and beyond our consciousness. And nothing can become the content of our knowing [*weten*] except the things that give themselves to our perceiving in advance. What we can in no way perceive, what gives rise to no awareness within us and does not enter into our consciousness, remains unknowable [*onkenbaar*] by the nature of the matter. We cannot even make proclamations about preexistence or nonexistence. Christian practitioners of science understood this very well when they unanimously recognized that all intellectual knowledge begins with perception; and Kant, with his "thoughts without content are empty" [*Begriffe ohne Anschauungen sind leer*],[3] would have met no objection from them.

3. Bavinck references Kant's theory of judgment from the *Critique of Pure Reason*: "Thoughts without content are empty, intuitions without content are blind."

But while, on the one side, science must remain on guard against the presumption that it possesses different organs of perception than the ordinary person, on the other side, it must also be on its guard against the drive to limit reliable perception and knowledge arbitrarily. In normal life, we all proceed silently from this, of which we are fully assured—not only of that which we see with our eyes and hear with our ears but also of all that rests on the testimony of our self-consciousness. We know that a visible world exists outside our consciousness; and with exactly the same—with no more, perhaps, but in any case also with no less—certainty, we know [*weten*] that there is a world of unseen things, a realm of the true, the good, and the beautiful. That lies enclosed in our self-awareness and is immediately given to us in our self-consciousness. We are not animals but humans—reasonable, moral, religious, aesthetic beings. The awareness of truth, goodness, and beauty is implanted in our nature; the distinction between true and untrue, between good and evil, between justice and injustice, between godless and pious [*godvruchtig*] is just as fixed in our consciousness as the distinction between light and dark, between day and night, between sour and sweet, between sound and silence, between use and destruction, between welcome and unwelcome. We would have to eliminate human nature itself if we wanted to rid ourselves of this awareness. Thus,

---

Immanuel Kant, *Critique of Pure Reason*, trans. and ed. Paul Guyer and Allen Wood (Cambridge: Cambridge University Press, 1998), 193–94.—Eds.

every person proceeds into life on the basis of awareness [of these unseen things]. They are already silently present in all his thinking and acting, and are the foundation of all his feeling and wanting. The family, society, state, religion, morality, law—the whole of history and the organization of humankind is built upon this awareness. And as such, science must also proceed from it.

Just as much as speculative rationalism [should be opposed], sensualism[4]—which arbitrarily limits perception, the knowledge of truth, and certainty, and is constantly in conflict with itself—should also be opposed. This is because it proceeds from the philosophical presupposition, which is acquired from thinking rather than sense perception, that all of our knowledge can be traced back to sensory impressions and is limited to this. It overlooks that, qualitatively, all sensory perception is just as much a psychical and very complicated activity as thinking and reasoning. It forgets that the psychical phenomena form a world in themselves and in the practice of life are, in fact, to the same extent as natural phenomena, a source of knowledge for all people.[5] It takes no account of [this],

4. Here Bavinck uses the uncommon term *sensrealisme*, which refers to the epistemological theory more commonly known as sensualism and associated with the French philosopher of mind Étienne Bonnot de Condillac (1714–1780). According to Condillac, all human faculties come from our sensations. See Lolke van der Zweep, *De pedagogiek van Bavinck, met een inleiding tot zijn werken* (Kampen: Kok, 1935), 194.—Eds.

5. "Sensualism is (also) certainly right in that, insofar as physical phenomena are taken into account, it regards sensory perception as the most original source, and final instance, of experience. On the one hand, however, it overlooks the fact that alongside the perception of psychical phenomena as experienced by the self, a second, no less reliable, source of experience flows, and that higher, i.e., more complex, psychical phenomena flow unnoticed into sensory perception." Wilhelm

that the psychical world is not simply a process of sensations and thoughts but, rather, in itself contains the witness of, points out, and unlocks the entrance to a wealth of ideas that are just as real and just as undeniable as the world that we see with our eyes and touch with our hands. And it places itself, thus, in an irresolvable tension with reality and life, with the facts of religion and morality, that it does not explain, [while it] rather destroys or otherwise gives preference to some hobbyhorse or arbitrariness.

Starting point, presupposition, and foundation are thus, in the last instance, the witness of our self-consciousness. Thus, the ineradicable awareness of a world lies enclosed within us and outside us, [a world] of soul and body, of mind and matter, of invisible and visible things.[6] Naturally, both of these worlds stand alongside

---

Jerusalem, *Einleitung in die Philosophie* (Vienna: Braumüller, 1899), 70. [Original German: "Der Sensualismus hat (auch) sicherlich darin Recht, dass er, so weit physische Phänomene in Betracht kommen, die Sinneswahrnehmung als ursprünglichste Quelle und letzte Instanz der Erfahrung ansieht. Er übersieht aber einerseits, dass daneben in der Beobachtung der selbst erlebten psychischen Phänomene eine zweite, nicht minder sichere Quelle der Erfahrung fliesst und dass in die sinnliche Wahrnehmung unbemerkt höhere, d.h. complicirtere psychische Phänomene mit einfliessen."]

6. Dr. Bruining is certainly correct when he says, in *Teyler's theologisch tijdschrift*, 1:318–19, that the acknowledgment of a world outside ourselves is not the product of a reasoning that [moves] from the existence of presuppositions to conclude with the existence of a cause external to us. And as such, in his view, we do not have to propose the psychical process. But "the representation comes to, so to speak, with the character of objectivity; or said differently, it arises as a representation of something external to us. And the difference between realism and idealism is now not that idealism remains with the representation and realism fixes something to it. To the contrary, realism takes the representation as it presents itself, while idealism deprives it of its original and proper character." Precisely the same applies, in a narrower sense, to psychical, religious, moral, aesthetical phenomena, which contain the reality of a world of invisible things, of a wealth of ideas. Whoever denies the latter cannot also maintain the former. [Here Bavinck refers to Albertus Bruining, "Over de methode van onze dogmatiek," *Teyler's theologisch tijdschrift* 1 (1903): 318–19n1.—Eds. Original Dutch: "De voorstelling komt tot ons, om het zoo uit te

each other as no less objective than subjective; their reality is confirmed for us in the singular and undivided self-consciousness; soul and body are most intimately united; the invisible things are revealed in the visible. We do not perceive the visible world through a psychical activity; it is the human mind that sees through the eye and hears through the ear. And because the mind is the actual agent here, and the senses are only used as organs, it can perceive and know the mind, the thought, the word in things. How the invisible things appear in the visible things, we do not know. What come to us from outside ourselves are, considered physically, nothing other than vibrations of light and ether that arouse the nerves of our senses. The manner in which these physical phenomena are symbols, guidelines, and bearers of thought and are able to work in our physical perceptions and representations is unknown to us. But the secret of this connection does not topple the fact: through the means of this connection we discover thought in the world, law in nature, order in the universe, beauty in the landscape, love in the eye, faithfulness in the heart. From all sides, representations impose themselves on our consciousness. They come to us along different paths, through eye and ear, through perceiving and thinking, through authority and reason,

---

drukken, met het teeken der objectiviteit; anders gezegd, zij treedt op als voorstelling van iets buiten ons. En het verschil tusschen realisme en idealisme is nu niet, dat het idealisme bij de voorstelling blijft staan en het realisme daaraan iets vastknoopt; omgekeerd, het realisme neemt de voorstelling, zooals zij zich geeft, terwijl het idealisme haar van een haar oorspronkelijk eigen karaktertrek ontdoet."]

through *ad fontes* investigation and tradition. They point back not only to a visible world that surrounds us but also to a wealth of ideas that comes to be revealed in the reasonable and moral nature of human beings. And therefore we are no indifferent observers; rather we value and judge, approve and reprove, wonder and condemn, love and hate. Therefore, we also make a distinction between true and false, sifting the representations that come to us, trying to work through them thoughtfully, and in science, setting for ourselves the goal of knowledge of the truth.

For all these reasons, scientific knowing does not stand in enmity against empirical knowing, or against the life upon which it is built. Rather, it rests upon it, proceeds from it, assumes it, and tries to purify it, to clarify it, and to expand it through intentional investigation and consideration. "The purpose of science is to expand and correct ordinary knowledge" [*Erweiterung und Berichtigung des gewöhnlichen Wissens ist der Zweck der Wissenschaft*].[7] Scientific research extends as far as

7. Julius Kaftan, *Die Wahrheit der christlichen Religion* (Basel: Detloff, 1889), 319. See also Herbert Spencer, *First Principles*, 5th ed. (London: Williams and Norgate, 1887), 18: "What is science? To see the absurdity of the prejudice against it, we need only remark, that science is simply a higher development of common knowledge; and that if science is repudiated, all knowledge must be repudiated along with it. The extremest bigot will not suspect any harm in the observation, that the sun rises earlier and sets later in the summer than in the winter, but will rather consider such an observation as a useful aid in fulfilling the duties of life. Well, astronomy is an organized body of similar observations, made with greater nicety, extended to a larger number of objects and so analyzed as to disclose the real arrangements of the heavens, and to dispel our false conceptions of them. That iron will rust in water, that wood will burn, that long kept viands become putrid the most timid sectarian will teach without alarm, as things useful to be known. But these are chemical truths: chemistry is a systematical collection of such facts, ascertained with precision, and so classified and generalized as to enable us to say with certainty, concerning each simple or compound substance,

empirical knowing. In daily life, we are aware not only of visible nature, which surrounds us, but also of a world of invisible things, of which we are citizens as reasonable and moral beings. That world is also the subject of scientific research and consideration, not to prove or deny its existence but to perceive and know its essence and laws. The setting of limits for science has a questionable side. All sorts of limits are indeed set for science, from the side of the subject, not only in the individual human being but in humanity. Our capacity to know is lacking and confused, our life is short, [and] our desire and energy are quickly exhausted. Absolute philosophy is a delusion, and progressivism, which believes in steady progress and, finally, in the establishment of a kingdom of truth here on earth, is a chiliastic dream. That we know [only] in part, shall remain the confession of the human being and humanity in this earthly dispensation. But it is still impossible to draw a circle in the world of phenomena within which exact science would be attainable and beyond which an "unknown land" [*terra incognita*] would expand endlessly. [This is] because it is difficult to say why the things outside the circle of exact science would be unknowable. Is it because they do not exist? But then the unknowability is self-evident, and the drawing of

what change will occur in it under given conditions. And thus is it with all the sciences. They severally germinate out of the experience of daily life; insensibly as they grow they draw in remoter, more numerous, and more complex experiences; and among these, they ascertain laws of dependence like this which make up our knowledge of the most familiar objects. Nowhere is it possible to draw a line and say—here science begins."

such a circle, wholly unnecessary and even nonsensical. Is it because they do indeed exist but are unknowable by their nature? If so, they must also be unthinkable and thus incomprehensible in their nature. Is it because they do indeed exist and are knowable, but our capacity for knowing is not equipped for them and cannot work them out? If so, it gives us a strange impression of a capacity for *knowing* that is equipped to make things that are defined, that exist, and that are thinkable—and that are of the highest importance to our life—*un*knowable to us. Kant and others have replied to this that God has intentionally created us as such, so that we would not know theoretically but should seek our goal in acting ethically. But this is a defective and moralizing answer. The question is, rather, why our capacity for knowing is equipped in such a strange way that we absolutely cannot know the things we would most want to know. After all, seeking the truth is no sin, and the truth is no lesser good than holiness and glory. Still, to say more, one can draw such borders, but nobody holds to them. Each person has his own "*metaphysisches Bedürfniss*" [metaphysical need]. Among the Greeks, science began with the deepest problems, with the questions of the cause, essence, and destiny of things, and on that basis it finally moved on to all people. What we seek and need for our life is a world-view that satisfies both our understanding [*verstand*] and our inner life [*gemoed*]. Such a worldview is built up not from details about visible nature alone but just as much from elements provided for us by our inner experience; it must bring unity in all our knowing [*kennen*] and acting, [bring] reconciliation between both our believing and our knowing [*weten*], and make peace between our head and our heart. We believe in that peace and seek it, because the truth cannot fight against itself, because our mind is one, because the world is one, because God is one. Even if the ideal is so far removed from us, the end goal of science can be none other than the knowledge of the truth—of the full, pure truth. That knowledge is never, and shall never be, a comprehending of how the human being should be able to find the Almighty fully. Rather, knowledge is something different from and higher than comprehending; it does not exclude mystery or chase away adoration. Alongside knowing, worship increases, because all science is the translation of the thoughts that God has laid down in his works. Pseudoscience can lead away from him, [but] true science leads back to him. In him alone, who is the truth itself, do we find rest, as much for our understanding [*verstand*] as for our heart. *In tota quippe, id est, in plena perfectione requies, in parte autem labor* [For rest is in the whole, i.e., in perfect completeness, while in the part there is labor].[8]

8. Augustine, *City of God* 11.31.

8

The Natural Sciences

Science, in general, and considered according to its idea [purpose], thus has the whole cosmos as its object and a systematized knowledge of it as its goal. It would first be complete and have reached its ideal when we would know the entirety of things in their final cause and goal, in their inner essence and connectedness. Science proceeds from philosophy. Alongside this, it also began historically. However, to the extent that research advanced and consideration was practiced, this one science was split into many particular sciences. The whole was there before the parts. From the whole, the members of the organism of science slowly grew and came to maturity. And this process of differentiation [*Differenzirung*] continues apace. At present, this one science is split into so many groups and subjects that its unity is often entirely forgotten, its practitioners are taken up in detailed studies, and the universities are fragmented into a complex of subject-specific schools. Thankfully, in recent years, eyes have been opened to the danger of this specialization, and the importance of the bond between the sciences [*vinculum scientiarum*], and in the study of philosophy, has been reawakened.

This unity should never be forgotten. Nonetheless, the division of science into a plurality of subjects is to be considered as a healthy, normal phenomenon. The field of research is so exceptionally broad and wide that division of labor is absolutely necessary. But alongside this, it should be central that each scientific discipline has the idea in common with science, considered in its entirety, and is a particular application of that idea. And this differs depending on the object that is presented to the research. The world is one whole and yet endlessly differentiated. Matter and spirit, nature and history, human and animal, soul and body, church and state, family and society, business and industry—these go together interdependently and stand alongside one another in all sorts of connections. But they are also distinguished from each other; each has its own character and nature, its own life and law. This unity-in-diversity should also be kept in view by the particular sciences. In the university, the unity of science and the idiosyncrasy of all the particular sciences must be treated properly. Only then does the school of higher learning [*hogeschool*] become a university of the sciences [*universitas scientiarum*]. Pantheistic fusion should be avoided, just as much as deistic disintegration.

From this, it immediately follows that there is no single method that is normal for all the sciences. Each particular science sets out its distinct demands in the inclination and tact of the researcher. There is a gift for studies in mathematics and physics, in literature and law, in history and philosophy. No one is suitable for everything, and not everyone is equally suitable for everything. There must be a relatedness between subject and object. Just as art is one and each particular art has its own idiosyncratic assumptions and demands, so too the unity of science does not exclude that every object of research distinguishes itself from all the others through one quality or other.

If this is so, then it is obvious that, depending on the character of the object that is being researched, there will also be a difference in the method of research, in the grounds upon which the knowledge rests, and in the certainty that can be reached. Not only between the so-called natural and mental sciences is there a difference in this regard, but also among the natural sciences. We recall but once that all science, including that of nature, rests upon metaphysical presuppositions and proceeds from general, self-establishing truths; obviously, no science can be imagined without accepting beforehand, quietly and without criticism, the reliability of the senses, the objective existence of the world, the truth of the laws of thinking, and the logical, ideal content of perceptible phenomena. And yet, while we allow this to go unspoken, we fix attention on [the fact] that between the disciplines of the natural sciences, there is a very great distinction, and that they can certainly not be fashioned according to one model. Since Kepler[1] and Newton,[2] the inclusion of astronomical phenomena within mathematics has slowly succeeded; and for a part, this has also been attained in physics, chemistry, and even in physiology. Jealous of the certainty that could be obtained here, those in other parts of the natural sciences have striven for such a mathematical certainty. There was, to the extent that one believed Oken,[3] only one certainty, namely, the mathematical; or according to Du Bois-Reymond,[4] there was no other knowing [*weten*] than the physical-mathematical.[5] Thus, in other sciences, for example in biology, the demand was made that phenomena should be explicable in mechanical-chemical terms. But while

1. Johannes Kepler (1571–1630), the German astronomer, mathematician, astrologer, and philosopher.—Eds.

2. Sir Isaac Newton (1642–1726/1727), the English mathematician, physicist, astronomer, theologian, and philosopher.—Eds.

3. Lorenz Oken (1779–1851), a German naturalist and botanist, tried to account for biology along mathematical lines. See Iain Hamilton Grant, *Philosophies of Nature after Schelling* (London: Bloomsbury, 2008), 94.—Eds.

4. Emile du Bois-Reymond (1818–1896), the German physiologist and brother of the mathematician Paul du Bois-Reymond (1831–1889). Emile was an early adopter of Darwinism in the German academy and advocated an extreme mechanistic materialism.—Eds.

5. Martin von Nathusius, *Das Wesen der Wissenschaft und ihre Anwendung auf die Religion: Empirische Grundlegung für die theologische Methodologie* (Leipzig: Hinrichs, 1885), 10.

this demand was maintained in principle, and the scientific ideal was sought in a mechanical explanation of the world, a weighty struggle on the limits of science quickly emerged from the naturalists. The relationships between organic beings were so complicated, [as] so many powers worked together [among them], that they could not be explained by a simple formula, such as a biogenetic law or natural selection. Haeckel[6] thus advanced one side [of the debate] and supplemented the details of experience with philosophical assumptions. In his 1878 lecture "The Current Day Theory of Evolution in Relation to Natural Science" [*Die heutige Entwickelungslehre im Verhältnisse zur Gesammtwissenschaft*],[7] in Stuttgart, he recognized that in exact and experimental terms his doctrine of the origination and development of organic beings was unprovable. [This was so] because all biological disciplines are, in the essence of the matter, *historical* and *philosophical* natural sciences. Although an exact mathematical demonstration for all sciences is to be entertained in principle, for the most part it is impossible to apply to the biological subjects. In place of an exact mathematical method here, the historical, the historical-philosophical, must come to their service.[8] Later, he more

6. Ernst Haeckel (1834–1919), a German philosopher, zoologist, eugenicist, and artist.—Eds.

7. Ernst Haeckel, *Die heutige Entwickelungslehre im Verhältnisse zur Gesammtwissenschaft. Rede auf der 50* (Munich: Amtlicher Bericht, 1877), 14–22. Versammlung Deutscher Naturforscher und Ärzte im München am 18. September 1877.

8. Martin von Nathusius, *Naturwissenschaft und Philosophie* (Heilbronn: Henninger, 1883), 42.

clearly supported his monistic philosophy,[9] which was based, despite his assertions, not on facts but rather on his own subjective convictions.

But others protested against this mixing of natural science and philosophy. Bastian[10] reproached Haeckel for wanting to give the theory a leading influence in our age of induction and experimentation, and accused him of betraying the holiest principle of our most sacred science.[11] Virchow[12] made a strong distinction between the speculative territory of the natural sciences and the [idea of the] factual mastery and completely firm terrain, and reckoned that the theory of descent belonged to the first terrain.[13] Du Bois-Reymond opposed the same confusion, trying to show the limits of natural science and counting no fewer than seven world puzzles that could not be resolved along the mechanical path.[14] Haeckel's *Riddle of the Universe* [*Welträthsel*] was later subjected to devastating criticism, not only by theologians and philosophers but also by natural scientists. And while Haeckel has re-

9. Ernst Haeckel, *Der Monismus als Band zwischen Religion und Wissenschaft* (Bonn: Strauss, 1893); Haeckel, *Die Welträthsel: Gemeinverständliche Studien über Monistische Philosophie* (Bonn: Strauss, 1899); cf. Albert Ladenburg, *Ueber den Einfluss der Naturwissenschaften auf die Weltanschauung* (Leipzig: Verlag von Veit, 1903).

10. Adolf Bastian (1826–1905), a nineteenth-century German polymath and a prominent critic of Haeckel.—Eds.

11. Adolf Bastian, *Offener Brief an Herrn Professor Dr. E. Häckel* (Berlin: Wiegandt, 1874).

12. Rudolf Virchow (1821–1902), a German intellectual known as the "father of modern pathology."—Eds.

13. Rudolf Virchow, *Die Freiheit der Wissenschaft im modernen Staat* (Berlin: Wiegandt, 1879).

14. Emile du Bois-Reymond, *Über die Grenzen des Naturerkennens: Die Sieben Welträthsel* (Berlin: Verlag von Veit, 1882).

turned to Spinoza, other natural scientists are currently aligning themselves with Leibniz. In quite broad circles, the mechanical explanation of the world is making room for the organic, the teleological, and in part, even for the theistic. Considering these facts, it is difficult to deny that natural science stands under the influence of a worldview, of philosophy, and thus also of faith or unbelief.[15] While it was first led in a certain direction in the nineteenth century by Hegel and Schelling, it then came under the domination of Darwinism and materialism, and now returns to the philosophy of Leibniz. And how could it be otherwise? Art, religion, state, society, law, [and] morality are always subject to the direction of the age; it is a miracle when the practitioners of science make an exception to this [rule]. They are also children of their age and cannot free themselves from their environment. That is not possible with regard to the perception and noting of phenomena, but it is much less applicable in seeking the law that governs the phenomena. Analysis is not enough for science. It must always be led and formed by synthesis. "Every analysis," says Goethe, "presupposes a synthesis.

15. This is no different in medical science. There it can be more sharply seen, because it owes its existence not to scientific principles but to practical needs. The medical faculty is composed of a number of disciplines that actually belong to the faculty of natural sciences but are united here for a practical goal, for the training of doctors and the healing of the ill. It thus bears an outstandingly empirical character. Nonetheless, throughout all of its history, it has been dominated by theories. A whole series of medical systems has arisen and then fallen away. It was so in Greece [and] in the Middle Ages, and [remains so] also in the modern age. In the current-day systems, older principles have returned. The newer means of healing, bathing, air, music, sunbathing, massage, hypnosis, therapeutic gymnastics, etc., are revivals of old methods. Some doctors insist, therefore, not wrongly, on the practice of the history of medicine.

A pile of sand cannot be analyzed, but if the pile contains grains of different materials [sand and gold, for instance], an analysis might be made by washing it: then the light grains will wash away and the heavy ones remain. Only together, like inhaling and exhaling, do both (analysis and synthesis) make up the 'life of science.'"[16]

Therefore, the practice of science needs not only a sharp view, a clear head, a diligent zeal, a good method, and a focused investigation. At the same time, it also demands a creative imagination, a gifted intuition, a surprising divination. This is the gift that, according to the history [*historie*] of science, has always brought a step forward. It has been the geniuses, not only in art but also in science, who have been given first place. Scientific discoveries come about not without, but also not only through, experimental investigation—and yet on the basis of this, through gifted "eureka moments" [*geniale "invallen"*]. Thousands have seen an apple fall, but the genius Newton discovered the law of gravity through it. At first, these moments are nothing but hypotheses, but these hypotheses—which have every right to exist in the practice of science and are even essential—lead to further investigation and point the way in the labyrinth of phenomena. If they are confirmed by the subsequent

16. "Jede Analyse . . . setzt eine Synthese voraus. Eiu Sandhaufen lässt zich nicht analysieren; bestünde er aber aus verschiedenen Theilen, man setze Sand und Gold, so ist das Waschen eine Analyse, wo das Leichte weggeschwemmt und das Schwere zurückbehalten wird. Nur beide zusammen (Analyse und Synthese), wie das Ausund Einatmen, machen das Leben der Wissenschaft." Goethe, cited in Nathusius, *Das Wesen der Wissenschaft*, 21.

perceptions, then they attain the rank of theories and laws. But however pleasing they are to us, they must also unrelentingly be given up if further investigation does not support them or overthrows them. So-called working hypotheses are only of value for as long as they explain facts. But it often happens that while they are only provisional in character, they are presented as established results of science or, also, that long after they have been deemed unsustainable, they are stubbornly entertained in the name of science. History [*geschiedenis*] is abundantly rich in examples in which the so-called undisputable results of science were played against religion and which, after a short period of growth, were themselves rejected after scientific advancement and fell into obscurity. Even the famous laws of nature seem not to be elevated beyond doubt. Radium, which was recently discovered, has provided the law of the conservation of energy with a hard test, and no one knows—so wrote someone recently, prompted by the new discovery—"what will be the fate of the iron laws laid down by the greatest minds of the nineteenth century as the final result of their penetration into the laws of nature."[17] In any case, from all this it seems sufficient [to say] that natural science cannot be cut loose from philosophy, from the influence of subjectivity, from the world-and-life view of the researcher. Next

17. Original: "was das Schicksal sein wird der ehernen Gesetze, die die grössten Geister des 19 Jahrhunderts als das Endergebniss des Eindringens in die Geheimnisse der Natur niedergelegt haben." *Die Woche*, January 2, 1904.

to love of neighbor, modesty is a virtue that also befits men of science. In mathesis, chemistry, [and] anatomy, the difference in life view may count for little; as soon as subjects like geology, palaeontology, biology, [and] anthropology come into view, faith and unbelief lay their weights on the scales.

9

The Humanities

This comes to the fore to a greater degree in the humanities. The rightness of the distinction between the natural sciences and the sciences of the humanities has not been deemed to be beyond discussion: the natural sciences very much have to deal with the invisible idea in the perceptible phenomena, and only come about because of the thought-work of the mind; and the humanities do not build up the truth through philosophical construction from the ideas of reason but are in their work, from start to finish, bound to perceptible phenomena; to manuscripts, monuments, products of art and literature; to historical and current institutions. And yet, be this as it may, in the present day the so-called humanities sciences are considered very idiosyncratic. Many hide shyly behind this and do not know what they are and what place they merit in [the world of] science. It goes without saying that if the method of the natural sciences, as it is mostly understood today, is the only true [method], the humanities either are no sciences at all or must submit themselves to the law of the natural sciences. Until that point [the phase of being subsumed under empirical sciences], the humanities had all moved, to borrow Comte's phrase once again, into their theological or metaphysical phase. Whoever no longer recognized God as the source of justice and law still accepted a source of moral intuitions in human nature, which laid the foundation for the humanities and set out a guideline in the practice thereof. But if all theology and metaphysics must be removed from science, the humanities—unless they wish to give up their existence—should also go over to the positive phase. And yet, it is no marvel that many are surprised at this consequence, because the prescribed change would entail nothing less than turning the humanities into the natural sciences. Therefore, there is a proposal that from now on, the humanities sciences should be retained alongside the natural sciences as "historical sciences" [*Geschichtswissenschaften*].[1]

1. Wilhelm Windelband, *Geschichte und Naturwissenschaft*, 2nd ed. (Strasbourg: Heitz, 1902) [a rectoral address reprinted in *Präludien: Aufsätze und Reden zur Philosophie und ihrer Geschichte*, vol. 2 (Tübingen: Mohr Siebeck, 1924), 130–60]; Heinrich Rickert, *Kulturwissenschaft und Naturwissenschaft* (Freiburg: Mohr, 1899); Rickert, *Die Grenzen der naturwissenschaftlichen Begriffsbildung*

This division deserves praise in that it perceives the distinction between nature and history, between empirical and historical method, and also wants to recognize and honor this important distinction in science. However, it cannot lay claim to being right because, first, the line between natural and historical science can only be drawn arbitrarily. Windelband[2] says that both differ formally; natural science seeks general laws, [and] historical science seeks particular facts; neither has as its goal the apodictic[3] or the assertoric;[4] in one, thought is nomothetic,[5] and in the other, idiographic.[6] But he himself must recognize, through reasoning, that one and the same object—as with, for example, geology, astronomy—can be handled nomothetically and idiographically. Each scientific discipline has a historical and a systematic part; natural science cannot miss the historical method in geology, paleontology, geography, and so on, and historical science in no way limits itself to the particular facts, but rather in those facts it seeks the idea that governs them.

Second, and following this, the aforementioned division leads to this [consequence]: that psychology be brought wholly into the natural sciences, and religion, ethics, law, and art be brought into historical science.

(Tübingen: Mohr, 1902). Rickert's latter work is discussed in Ernst Troeltsch, *Theologische Rundschau* (1903), 3–27, 57–71.

2. Wilhelm Windelband (1848–1915), a German philosopher.—Eds.

3. *Apodictic*: clearly established or beyond dispute.—Eds.

4. *Assertoric*: relating to a logical assertion that something is true.—Eds.

5. *Nomothetic*: relating to the discovery of general scientific laws.—Eds.

6. *Idiographic*: relating to the discovery of particular scientific facts and laws.—Eds.

With this, violence is done to psychology, because just as there is an unmistakable bond between the physical and the psychical, it is just as sure that they are different in essence. This profound difference is overlooked when psychology is incorporated into the natural sciences. But when this difference in the division of psychology is not taken into account, it cannot be decisive in the grouping of those subjects that deal with religion, ethics, art, and literature. If one replies that the proposed division, however it is called, is defined not by the character of the object but strictly and only through the following of the empirical or the historical method, then not only does the objection arise, which was just named in the first place, but one also forgets that the method is defined precisely by the character of the object.

Third, and more urgent still, is the concern that if the sciences that have as their content religion, ethics, law, and so on may only apply the historical method, they will at once lose their normative character. Natural science can trace out laws; it may proceed nomothetically. But historical science, according to Windelband, has the task of "bringing to a full and exhaustive presentation" [*zu voller und erschöpfender Darstellung zu bringen*] religious, ethical, and aesthetic phenomena; it only adds lucidity and is satisfied by describing the full richness of human life, such as that of religion, morality, law, language, [and] art in the present day, in a vivid manner. Naturally, all right to judgment and appreciation is lost, or at the most it retains only a subjective character. Faith and unbelief, piety and godlessness, love and hate, justice and injustice, good and evil, truth and lies—all have an equal right to exist; they all have their place in the passage of history; there is no more absolute standard of measure.[7] These sciences no longer say what should count as religion, ethics, law, and so forth, what has counted for such until the present day.

But, finally, the aforementioned sciences cannot remain as described here. One might well wish [they could], but this is a striving for something unattainable. Everyone expects of these sciences that they will say what should count as religion, ethics, and law, for every person. The nature and the life of the human being is too strong for him to be able to silence this expectation. According to the classical view, philosophy stands in the closest connection to life wisdom. And even if people did not expect this of the sciences in question, they themselves could not escape this requirement, because science is the doing of truth. Reality is not enough for it; it wants truth and, along with that, norms, law, and authority. This is seen in the strivings of those who want to make all science positive and historical. However, because they have given up the absolute measure with which to judge good and evil, they try to borrow details from history and statistics that determine what should be held as truth, justice, morality,

---

7. Compare also J. M. J. Valeton, *Het Oud-Romeinsche huwelijk in het licht van het zedelijk oordeel* (Amsterdam: De Bussy, 1903).

and so on, in the future. "The greatest happiness of the greatest number" then becomes the norm for religion and morality, for logic and aesthetics. Considered on its own, everything is a "private matter" [*Privatsache*], a question of preference and taste, of character and upbringing.

But as this principle would lead to unfettered arbitrariness, individualism must be subdued by socialism. Science, represented in an Areopagus of the learned, must thus define and fix for everyone, on the basis of historical and statistical details, what has the right to be considered truth and justice. It has the highest authority. In the past, church and state, religion and priesthood governed humanity; but now it is science's turn to arise as the "benefactor of the people and liberator of humanity" [*Wohlthäterin der Völker und Befreierin der Menschheit*].[8] It must make its declarations with the authority of dogmata that determine the doctrine and life of human beings.[9] On the basis of historical [*historische*] and statistical details, it must establish whether monotheism or polytheism, whether truth or lies, whether marriage or free love deserves preference. The only power that has the privilege of commanding faith and obedience, says Clavel, is "the scientific law" [*la loi scientifique*]. "No one rejects it, if he is not an idiot" [*Nul ne la repousse, s'il n'est idiot*]. On the basis of facts, the science of ethics must establish for the family, the people,

8. A. Malvert, *Wissenschaft und Religion* (Frankfurt: Neuer Frankfurter, 1904), 124.

9. Ludwig Stein, *Die soziale Frage im Lichte der Philosophie: Vorlesungen über Sozialphilosophie und ihre Geschichte* (Stuttgart: Enke, 1903), 533.

and humanity what is good and what must be obeyed by all.[10] If society finds more advantage in lies than in the truth, their places would have to be switched, because the human being does not exist for the truth, but rather the truth for the human being, just as it comes from him and by him.[11] The eternity of moral laws exists in their eternal becoming.[12] According to some, [to ensure] that its social instincts are followed, the state must, if necessary, force people with violence.

Thus positivism, applied to the humanities, leads not only to undermining the foundations of human life but also to a scientific hierarchy that threatens our freedom in a very serious way. And this hierarchy is all the more unbecoming here, because ultimately, it proceeds on the basis of nothing but arbitrariness. It is easy to perceive that the positive, empirical method is not suitable for application in the humanities. It has even been shipwrecked in the natural sciences, because only the connection of analysis and synthesis leads to science. But in the humanities, its application is equivalent to the destruction of those sciences. In principle, this is not agreed upon by all those who divide science into natural and historical science and, as such, still entertain the empirical method alongside the historical. But insofar as this historical method

10. Adolphe-Charles Clavel, *La morale positive* (Paris: Bailliere, 1873), 53, 78, 203.

11. Rudolf von Jhering, *Der Zweck im Recht*, vol. 2 (Leipzig: Breitkopf & Härtel, 1886), 588.

12. Wilhelm Wundt, *Ethik* (Stuttgart: Enke, 1886), 442.

truly distinguishes itself from the empirical method, such a certainty cannot be obtained within the humanities, as [it] can be, to a certain extent, in the natural sciences. History [*historie*] always rests on fallible human witnesses, who, in all critique, must ultimately be accepted by faith; it can thus never lead to a mathematical certainty.[13] It follows from this that in history [*geschiedenis*], we enter a terrain that is not governed by the laws of nature, but where the personality and freedom of the human being make their influence count. There are indeed historians who apply the empirical method on this terrain and try to discover fixed laws of nature; but this striving is hardly met with favorable results. The laws that one first thought to have found in religion, ethics, [and] art, in the development of state and society, are many, but that ongoing research has shown to be worthless and to be not much more than a certain typical regularity and rhythmic periodicity repeated in events.[14] Therefore there are also those who challenge the scientific character of history, and even regard education in this subject to be ineffective and of little fruit.[15]

The humanities are then only to be maintained in their independence, proceeding as they do from the intuitions

---

13. J. G. R. Acquoy, *Handleiding tot de kerkgeschiedvorsching en kerkgeschiedschrijving* (The Hague: Nijhoff, 1894), 79. [Acquoy] speaks too strongly of "evidentness."

14. Compare, for example, the sociological laws in Rudolf Eisler, *Soziologie: Die Lehre von der Entstehung und Entwicklung der menschlichen Gesellschaft* (Leipzig: Weber, 1903), 12–16.

15. For example, Alfred Fouilée; cf. *Wetenshappelijke Bladen* (September 1901): 441–49.

of truth, ethics, and justice that are given in our nature. In a certain sense the objects of natural science are present to us only in the form of representations in our own consciousness. We can never come close to the world outside us, other than through our representations. And yet, there is, just as was noted above, a great difference. While the natural sciences always strive for knowledge of the outside world through our representations, the humanities have as their content "the immediate experience as determined by the interaction of objects with knowing and acting subjects" [*die unmittelbare Erfahrung, wie sie durch die Wechselwirkung der Objekte mit erkennenden und handelnden Subjekten bestimmt wird.*].[16] For the humanities, the objects of representation and subjective movements led by them count as immediate reality, and they seek to account for these in their origin and essence. This should not be understood in the sense of psychologism, as though the humanities were nothing other than sciences of consciousness and thus should be seen as components of psychology. This is so because, while—like all science—their roots lie in the life of the soul, they strive for a knowledge of the reality that objectively exists but exists only psychically and therefore can only be perceived and known by our psyche. In philology, history, and philosophy, in the doctrines of law, the state, and fellowship, one is always concerned with the knowledge of

16. Wilhelm Wundt, *Psychologie*, 2nd ed. (Leipzig: Engelmann, 1897), 4.

the human being according to his inner, invisible, spiritual side. And yet, this is not only the knowledge of what he is, but, further, just as with medical science, it concerns the knowledge of what he should be as an individual and socially, in family and state. None of these sciences has only a historical goal. Each also has a systematic goal. But they cannot fulfill this task without proceeding from the truth of those intuitions that are given in human nature. Philology is not possible without the presupposition that language hides the logos. History cannot be practiced without the prior foundation that events are governed by an idea and are led to a goal. Psychology can only be maintained in its independence when psychical phenomena differ in essence from physical phenomena. Ethics and aesthetics lose their scientific character when the norms of good and evil, of beauty and ugliness are given up. And jurisprudence loses its place of honor when it does not possess any standard by which to measure justice and cannot test the laws of the day.

It is true that these sciences are not speculative sciences that build up language and ethics, justice and law, state and society, from a priori principles. They are very much bound to the psychical world, just as it reveals itself in all of these phenomena. Jurisprudence investigates the law of the day and finds there its material and object. And such is the case with all the humanities sciences; in a certain sense they are positive, which is to say, they find their objects presented to them in the real world. Even philosophy loses itself in idle speculations when it despises this given reality. In order to get to know and to judge the psychical world that exists beyond ourselves, we need the witness of our consciousness, of our own psychical existence, of our soul's intuitions, and [we need] to proceed from the reality of ideas posited therein. There are also no other sources of knowledge open to the humanities than the normal, empirical laws upon which the psychical world is built. If it despises these, it dooms itself to fruitlessness, calls for a doomed conflict in life, and works toward its own failure. Family, state and society, language, [and] law and morality are grounded in these intuitions of the soul.

Naturally, this is not to say that science should simply bow down, without critique, before all that exists. But to engage in critique on what exists, true and pure critique, it must possess a standard that is not susceptible to being scaled down or expanded. And this is provided in the witness of our consciousness. Here, regardless of whether he wants to, every person recognizes a truth, goodness, and beauty that proceeds far above empirical reality. Each person is a citizen of a kingdom other than the kingdom of nature; he is subject to a moral world order; he is a reasonable and moral being and cannot and may not free himself from himself. Herein lies the essence, the greatness, the glory of the human being. The more we consider the higher nature of the human, the more we—like Kant—are filled with wonder for it. And each concern with proceeding from its reality melts like snow before the sun. After all, if we cannot believe ourselves in this regard, what reason would we have to accept the witness of our consciousness with regard to the world outside ourselves? All humanities sciences rest especially on the inner intuition of the soul, on the deepest conviction, on the nobility of our human nature, on the majesty of the subject, just as the minister of internal affairs recently said in the Second Chamber.[17] And only so can science, not in place of but alongside religion, be of benefit to humanity if it recognizes the human being's reasonable and moral nature and builds upon this in faith.

17. Here Bavinck refers to Abraham Kuyper, at that time minister of internal affairs, alongside his role as prime minister.—Eds.

10

Theological Science

With theology, which in this last place asks for a few moments of our attention, this all comes more clearly into the light. Impressed by Kant's critique of the capacity for knowing, and out of fear for the resolute language of modern science, many have allowed themselves to be lured to a dangerous concession. They have conceded that there was no knowledge of God to be obtained, and that, as such, theology has no right to the name of science. They have insisted that the faculty of theology should be turned into a faculty of religious science, and have seen their wishes fulfilled in the Higher Education Act of 1876.[1] The

1. The Higher Education Act was a piece of legislation that required the Netherlands' theological faculties to become faculties of religious studies, albeit while

proponents of this change were all sincerely convinced that they had protected the independent scientific character of theology from all attacks by giving it the knowledge of religion, but not the knowledge of God, as its object. Religion is a phenomenon in human history the existence and significance of which can be denied by no one.

This last point is completely correct; but a different question concerns whether religious science is justified in being an independent faculty. Judging by the tone taken by the civilized and cultured who often make pronouncements on this new science, and by the posture that they take toward it, one cannot say that the change has been good for it or that its honor has been advanced. Many men of science find it unusually pleasing that professional theologians make it so easy for them in their fight against the Christian faith; but a hearty recognition of the good rights of religion is seldom heard from their lips. Certainly, the history of religions can rejoice in the particular interest [it now receives], but as soon as one attempts to move from the history of religions to a religion applied to the present day, this interest makes way for indifference, sometimes even for mocking despisal. The civilized are just as poorly served by modern religion and theology as the common folk. Theology's scientific reputation has

retaining the name *theology* (*godgeleerdheid*). Bavinck was a theological student at the University of Leiden when this law was implemented. See James Eglinton, *Bavinck: A Critical Biography* (Grand Rapids, MI: Baker Academic, 2020), 89–90.—Eds.

not increased very much through its metamorphosis into religious science.

This is not difficult to understand, because the transformation only took place partially and gave the impression, to the left and to the right, of being somewhat half-hearted. The combination of subjects arranged by the Higher Education Act provides convincing proof of this. In part, these are subjects from the old faculty of theology, and in part, they have been borrowed from the new faculty of religious science; and this confusion has been crowned by this, that the new ship sails under the old flag; the newly styled faculty is religious science and wishes to be this, but it still bears the name of theology. The half-hearted character of religious science comes across no less strongly in the task that it takes upon itself and the goal that it intends. It is not exclusively the study of the history of religions, but, rather, through that study it intends to arrive at the knowledge of the origin and essence of religion. Beginning with history, it nonetheless proceeds toward dogmatics, a philosophy of religion, and an ethic. But according to the current-day conception of science, as we have already seen, there is only room for the empirical and, closest to it, the historical method. There can be no such thing as dogmatics, which brings truth into the light, according to the understanding of science held by many. If religious science nonetheless wants to move toward this, in that very moment it gives up its scientific character—the maintenance of which was the reason for its metamorphosis. The path of pure empiricism and historicism cannot lead to dogma regarding religion. If religious science moves—and wants to move—in that direction, only this can be said: it proceeds not from the fact of religion but from a certain valuation of that fact. If it was only a matter of the knowledge of the historical phenomenon of religion, its study could and should be brought under the faculty of literature. If it wants to be an independent faculty, then the heart of the matter is that it does not treat religion purely as a historical phenomenon. It proceeds from the presupposition that religion is not just a historical reality but, rather, objective truth; not a delusion, not an imagining, not mental illness but a necessary detail of human nature, an idiosyncrasy, a virtue, that pertains to the essence of the human, that has a right to exist.

This presupposition is now so weighty and so rich in content that, in formal terms, the modern theologians have no reason to treat their own neutral scientific approach haughtily while looking down on the orthodox as those who anxiously lock themselves up in their dogma. This is so because this presupposition is nothing other than one dogma—principial, all-dominating, binding the entirety of science in advance. What is not contained within it? If religion is objective truth, then it is clear that religions that emerge among humankind cannot all be true to the same degree. Religions have this idiosyncratic quality, distinct from, for example, languages, in that they stand directly opposed to one another, in that one regards as lies what another counts as truth, and in that they judge and strive against each other, even to the shedding of blood. In spite of its purported tolerance, modern religion is no exception in this regard. It might assert, absent-mindedly, that all religions are forms of the revelation of one religion, that none of them possesses the whole truth, that life rather than doctrine is the key issue; in practice it fights the Roman and the Reformed, churches and confessions, among others, with equal strength, just as every religious persuasion does to the others. And this can only be so. If someone is convinced in his soul of the truth of his own confession, he cannot find rest and peace in a different confession that strives against it, because religion is always a matter of the highest good for the human being; it is woven into his most inner being and cannot be neutral. Orthodoxy and modernism cannot both be equally true; if the first is right, the other is wrong; and vice versa. Modern theology not only proceeds from the presupposition that religion in general is objective truth; it also honors a certain view of religion and has its own religion. It confesses that its religion is true and that it is revealed in the different forms of religion, goes through a process of development in them, and in Christianity, then in the Reformation and now, finally, has found its purest expression in the religion of the moderns. Now, it does not matter at this point in our argument whether the modern religion is capable of leading to a more or less circumscribed confession, to a churchly organization, or to its own cult. If necessary, in the view of the Romantics, let them exist in nothing but a mood and be cut loose of all representation and action—something that no modern theologian will assert in an absolute sense, and that is also impossible in itself. Considered as such, modern theology also represents its own view of religion. It believes not only in the truth of religion in general; it is also convinced that the view of religion that it honors is the true one—in other words, that in its eyes, all forms of religion are deficient and impure, and that its religion is the purest and highest of all.

But in the presupposition upon which the faculty of religious science is built, something else, of more consequence, is contained. If we do not wish to play with words but give our earnest consideration to the content of our confession, then [we] understand that faith in God, in his personal existence, is also contained in faith in the objective truth of religion. This is undeniable: if there is no God, then religion—the serving of God[2]—is foolishness; and vice versa, if religion is truth, the existence of God is established at the same time. Theology, in the sense of the knowledge of God, is the heart of religion. If religious science does not wish to be purely empirical and historical—in which case, it would be at home in the

2. The Dutch term *godsdienst* (religion) means literally "service of God." In Bavinck's text, this line ("als er geen God is, is godsdienst, is dienen van God dwaasheid") draws out the blunt meaning of *godsdienst* to readers who might gloss over its etymology.—Eds.

faculty of literature—but wants instead to arrive at the knowledge of religion along the path of empirical and historical investigation, it then presupposes the truth of religion and, in so doing, the necessity of the existence of God. Furthermore, the knowability of God cannot be separated from that divine existence, which is accepted in and with the truth of religion; because a God who can in no sense be known is, in practical terms for us, the same as a God who does not exist. And finally, if God is knowable, to whatever weak degree, then it is not only the case that he has revealed himself, because what we absolutely cannot perceive, we also cannot know; and what we in no sense can know, we also cannot love and serve. Modern religious science, which, as a particular faculty, rests on the presupposition of the truth of religion, simultaneously accepts in advance the existence, the revelation, and the knowability of God. In other words, it keeps one foot in metaphysics and has only partially outgrown supernaturalism. Incidentally, naturalism and religion cannot be united. All religion is supernaturalistic [in that it] assumes that God is transcendent above the world, [that he] is different from the world in essence, and that he is conscious of the world and reveals himself, even if only in the inner life of the pious. The prayer for a pure heart, Pierson has rightly said, is just as supernaturalistic as the sick man's prayer for recovery.[3]

---

3. Allard Pierson, *Gods wondermacht en ons geestelijk leven* (Arnhem: Thieme, 1867), 42.

Formally, in all of this, there is no difference between the moderns and the orthodox. There is no science of religion *in general* unless God exists, is knowable, and has revealed himself. It is thus untrue and superficial if one person says to another, "You are dogmatic, but we are scientific; you are prejudiced and sectarian, but in my research I set to work wholly objectively and accept nothing other than by evidence." Neither does the argument hold if the same accuser would rather say, "It is true that I move forward from some presuppositions, but while you hold on to your presuppositions to the end, despite all the results of science, I consider mine only to be working hypotheses and am prepared to give them up as soon as science shows their untenability."

If those presuppositions are simply working hypotheses, which do not seem to hang together with religious life, then the orthodox will just as gladly and willingly give them up as the moderns. Naturally, neither will do this as soon as the first and most learned lets his voice be heard. He will weigh it, test, and investigate. Whoever inspects the history of science, if only in the last century, learns not to be afraid at the first rumor [of a scientific breakthrough]; he stays calm regarding the so-called results of science and becomes steadily more convinced of their human weakness and fallibility. But if they are really and truly the results of science, the orthodox accepts them just as gladly as the moderns. There is no one who does not gratefully recognize and enjoy the discoveries and inventions of science in the previous century. Not a single man of science feels his conscience bound to working hypotheses.

But the issue becomes wholly different when the presuppositions from which our scientific research proceeds are not working hypotheses but convictions that are rooted in the depths of our soul and grow together with our most intimate life. As long as a person maintains this, he cannot simultaneously regard them as working hypotheses that he is prepared to give up because of the outcomes of scientific investigations. Whoever says with Asaph,[4] "Whom have I in heaven besides you? / There is nothing on earth that I desire besides you" cannot also say, "This faith is only a working hypothesis; I will give it up, as soon as science demonstrates to me that it is untenable." And if he were to speak as such, he would show that he did not truly believe and was only a pretender. In this regard, there is no difference between Roman Catholics and Protestants, moderns and orthodox. None who value religion and find their highest blessedness in fellowship with God can be neutral and objective regarding all that science is pleased to declare. Rather, they will all say with one voice: "Science cannot take what I possess in the depths of my inner life, which is most tender and holy, away from me. Science must keep its distance from it, because it lies beyond science's terrain. And if science

4. Bavinck is citing Ps. 73:25, in a psalm of Asaph.—Eds.

nonetheless does this, it goes beyond what it is qualified to do, betrays itself, and becomes a false science. Thousands of learned people and all the men of repute in the present day might say to me that my faith is foolishness. [In response to] the science that is fashionable today, I call upon the science that has endured through the ages."

That is the language of faith, and so speak all those for whom religion remains objective truth. Naturally, this is not to say that such people are closed to any change of conviction. Although it is normal that someone dies in the religion of his upbringing, on the mission field and in the established churches all sorts of conversions are taking place. Roman Catholics become Protestants, and vice versa; moderns see their numbers strengthened from orthodox circles. But of what character are these conversions? Are they the same as the changes in the realm of science, when one hypothesis is exchanged for another, when it seems unsustainable? No one shall dare to claim that. When a Roman Catholic steps over to the Protestant religion, when a modern moves over to the orthodox confession—when such a change happens in full subjective earnestness and from conviction—that is the consequence of a religious-moral crisis that has taken place in the deepest part of the life of his soul. The Christian who is taught by the Scriptures even confesses that no one comes to faith in Christ as his Savior and Lord unless he is born of God. The natural man does not understand the things that are of God. To see the kingdom of heaven, one must be born again of water and of Spirit. And whoever then leaves the Christian church shows by this that he never was in the truth or belonged to it. The character of this change proves that religion is wholly different from science. Testing out a new working hypothesis has nothing to do with the moral change by which religion brings us to a new confession. They are as different as can be. Everyone gladly wants to give up prejudices when he becomes better informed. But in truth, there is no religious person who wants to see his religious and ethical convictions listed as prejudices. He cannot and may not do this as long as he embraces them with all his soul. How much more than his scientific name and honor is he prepared to offer his goods and life, if necessary, for the fellowship with God sought by every man in his religion. The blessing and woe of humanity depend on religion. To lose one's soul is to lose everything.

11

Revelation

Formally, there is then no difference in the posture that the religious man takes, and must take, from [the posture] of the scientific man. [When someone] believes in religion, and thus in the existence, the revelation, and the knowability of God, [that belief] must demand that intellect and heart, faith and science should live together in peace. He must strive for an *einheitliche* [unified] worldview, in which room is made not only for science but also for religion. However, coupled with that formal agreement, there is a great material difference. The question that divides religions and confessions is this: Where is the revelation of God to be found, from which we are able to know him, and which is thus the source of religion?

Although in previous ages, people considered the whole world as a revelation of God, this revelation has been increasingly limited since the eighteenth century. Rationalism blurred the history and content of revelation into a few general, abstract truths of reason. In turn, this rationalism was undermined by Kant and Schleiermacher.[1] In his *Critique of Pure Reason*,[2] the former concluded that if we were only *knowing* beings, we could know nothing certain about God, the soul, freedom, or immortality. He was particularly pleased with this result and believed that he had rendered a great service to the cause of religion, morality, and theology by making them independent of rational proofs. He was a witness of how weakly rationalist theology performed in the past in the face of attacks from empiricism, and how it had continually lost ground—[all of which] Kant looked upon with anguished eyes. It brought him great delight that, according to the demand of his conscience, he had found another, firmer foundation for morality, theology, and religion. He thus gladly gave up knowing [*het weten*] because, and so that, alongside and independently of knowing, he could retain an unassailable place for faith. Morality then became the foundation and, in

1. Friedrich Schleiermacher (1768–1834), the Prussian theologian best known as the "father of modern theology."—Eds.

2. Immanuel Kant, *Critique of Pure Reason*, trans. and ed. Paul Guyer and Allen Wood (Cambridge: Cambridge University Press, 1998).—Eds.

connection to the idea of God he derived from it, also the content of religion.

Starting from wholly other premises, Schleiermacher came to a similar result. He also regarded the absolute, which is exalted above all antitheses, as unknowable to the human intellect, which always deals in antitheses. But while Kant subsequently placed the revelation of God mainly within the categorical imperative and the commandments of the moral law, Schleiermacher expressed the view that the absolute could be experienced only in feeling [*het gevoel*]. [In Kant], religion primarily consisted of moral action; [in Schleiermacher,] in the affections of the inner life. These ethical and mystical views played a prominent role in the theology of the nineteenth century. Now, however, the latter position is increasingly displacing the former. Alongside this, the neo-Kantianism of Ritschl[3] has already had its day. Among others, younger theologians bring this objection to Ritschl: that he has allowed religion to be too one-sidedly absorbed into ethics, and that he has had no eye for its mystical [side]. Ritschl has failed to do justice to Schleiermacher—an error that must be corrected. Religion is nothing but personal piety, an *Erlebniss* [experience] of the soul, an affection of the inner life, which is only experienced between God and the individual soul. Before all else, it touches the personal, the secretive, the mystical. The enthusiasts, the

3. Albrecht Ritschl (1822–1889), a German Protestant theologian.—Eds.

ecstatic, and the apocalyptics are the actual and true religious [followers]. With some bias, they are dug up from history and set on stage. And this is not only so of theologians. Literary scholars, historians, and artists also occupy themselves with these [religious mystics]. Just as art must be studied from the works of masters, so must one come to know the essence of religion from its seers and prophets. It is not religion's content that matters but only its primordial, personal power. And while religion is entirely blended into moods and affections of the inner life, we can quietly give up nature and history, art and science—theology included—to secularization. [In this view,] religion has nothing to do with theology, which must simply become a historical science like any other.[4]

This view is consistent indeed. There is no conclusion from which it shrinks back. However, it rests on a total misunderstanding of the essence of religion. For all religion can make claims to truth if—and indeed only exists as long as—its confessors are convinced of that truth. The affections that religion fosters in the human soul die off as soon as its objective truth no longer stands firm for the faith. The neoromantic view of religion does not

4. See, among others, Bernhard Duhm, *Das Geheimniss in der Religion* (Leipzig: Mohr, 1896); Arthur Bonus, *Religion als Schöpfung* (Leipzig: Eugen Diederichs, 1902); Friedrich Naumann, *Briefe über Religion* (Berlin: Buchverlag der Hilfe, 1903). Religion is nothing other than a certain experience and mood of the soul: "God and the soul, the soul and its God" (*Gott und die Seele, die Seele und ihr Gott*). Everything objective and historical is outside the way of religion. This is also so in the views of religion found in Harnack and Sabatier. The consequence of this is that insofar as theology wants to be a science, it must become the science of religion and only bear a personal and practical character. In essence, this is also the case with Lagarde, Overbeck, Bernoulli, Troeltsch, Gross, et. al.

take these essential elements into account, and gives the appearance that religion has nothing to do with truth and morality and, rather, spontaneously blossoms from the inner life of man. Religion then becomes a question of taste, a private matter, a pastime for those whose natures are so disposed, the consideration of which gives others aesthetic delight. There can be no talk of a revelation of God in nature and history, which would lie as the foundation of religion. At the most, only in the deepest part of the human essence is there a [feeling that is] affected by the infinite, an "immediate feeling of the infinite and eternal" [*unmittelbares Gefühl des Unendlichen und Ewigen*], a "desire and taste for the infinite" [*Sinn und Geschmack für das Unendliche*], which is interpreted and represented by the different religions, and especially by the virtuosos of religion, each in his own manner. These representations are entirely subjective and make no claim to truth; they have value only insofar as they give striking expression to the moods of the heart. The ideal, then, is that all religions should mutually embrace and that, as in the parliament in Chicago,[5] Christians, Muslims, Buddhists, and so on would shake hands as brothers.

It is no wonder that a reaction to this syncretism is emerging. Here in the Netherlands, some moderns are taking up a degree of zeal for Christian theism, for the right of metaphysics, for personal immortality, and in

5. Bavinck is referring to the Parliament of the World's Religions, a major interfaith event held in Chicago in 1893.—Eds.

part for the doctrine of Christ. And in Germany there are more and more voices against Haeckel and Ladenburg,[6] who also acknowledge a revelation of God in nature and history and thus advocate the harmony of religion and science.[7] Whoever is serious about religion cannot limit revelation to a mystical working of the infinite in the human inner life. The human being is not isolated in the world. He is bound to his environment with every fiber of his being. Like someone who is hungry but will take no food from outside himself and thus starves to death, so is the religious man who isolates himself from the world and must live off his own inner affections [*gemoedsaan-*

---

6. Albert Ladenburg (1842–1911), a German chemist, rejected all Christian dogmas and regarded the French Revolution as more beneficial to humankind than the advent of Christianity. See Herman Bavinck, *Reformed Dogmatics*, ed. John Bolt, trans. John Vriend, vol. 1, *Prolegomena* (Grand Rapids, MI: Baker Academic, 2003), 258—Eds.

7. Compare, for example, Ferdinand Brunetière, *La science et la religion* (Paris: Firmin-Didot, 1895); George John Romanes, *Thoughts on Religion* (London: Longmans, Green, 1896); Johannes Reinke, who had already expressed himself in his work *Die Welt als Tat*, recently gave a lecture in the Berlin Evangelical Union on the question "Is nature as revelation of God valid? An affirmative answer" (*Beweis des Glaubens*, [February 1904]: 64); Johannes Classen, *Naturwissenschaftliche Erkenntnis und der Glaube an Gott* (Hamburg: Boysen, 1903); Richard Bärwinkel, *Verträgt sich die Naturwissenschaft mit dem Gottesglauben? Ein Wort gegen Ladenburg und Haeckel* (Leipzig, 1904); Hermann Schell, *Der Gottesglaube und die naturwissenschaftliche Welterkenntnis* (Bamberg: Schmidt, 1904); Arthur Titius, *Religion und Naturwissenschaft: Eine Antwort an Professor Ladenburg* (Tübingen: Mohr, 1904), etc.

At the end of his essay "The Zeeman Effect" ("Het Zeemanverschijnsel," *De Gids* 67 [March 1903]), Prof. Van der Waals said that everything in nature is the realization of an all-encompassing and yet indivisible divine idea. Behind everything, there is a highly exalted intellect, for there are laws and rules everywhere. [Johannes van der Waals (1837–1923) was a Dutch theoretical physicist and Nobel Prize winner.—Eds.] And Prof. Bakhuis Roozeboom concluded his address "The Current State of the Problems of Chemistry" ("De tegenwoordige stand van de problemen der chemie" [Leiden 1904]) with these words: "The further we penetrate into the knowledge of the still unknown domains, the more cause there shall be for the admiration of the divine world order, which also reveals itself in this field of nature and which leads from manifold diversity back to a few basic principles." [Hendrik Willem Bakhuis Roozeboom (1854–1907) was a Dutch chemist.—Eds.]

doeningen], impoverished. Thus, all those for whom religion is a matter of the heart have always thought about this differently. To them, nature and history are a revelation of God. To them, the whole world is a proclamation of his virtues. Now, if this were not mere delusion and imagination but indeed the correct view, then at the foundation there must be a revelation of God in all his works. And this cannot be otherwise, because one of two things [must be the case]: either the world is not a revelation of God and, as such, cannot be his work and owes its origin to something other than God, or it is indeed his work in both origin and progress, and must also, to some degree, make us to know [*kennen*] his essence.

However, if God reveals himself in all his works, it then goes without saying that this revelation cannot be the same in manner and content in every part and point of the world. The world is always an organic whole and displays, in the richest diversity, its unity. God's wisdom and omnipotence, his goodness and holiness are revealed, to varying degrees, in the creatures—more in organic life than in the inorganic, and also in rational [creatures], his revelation appears differently and more richly than in the irrational. In history, in particular, we—individual persons as much as humanity—come into contact with antitheses that cannot be retraced to God in the same sense. However much monism tries to insert evil as a necessary moment of development in the world as a whole, the religious-moral consciousness continues to maintain the antithetical character of truth and lies, holiness and sin, righteousness and guilt. Sin may not circumvent the governance of God, and yet [it] is not his work in the way that the good is. And this antithesis also applies to the field of religions. It is simple pantheistic monism that takes all of these [things] as links in a single chain, as moments in a process, as revelations of the same God that differ only in degree and scope. Precisely because there is no religion without ideas, the religions exist not as steps above [or below one another] but antithetically, adjacently to each other. Whoever erases this contrast not only fails to do justice to the religions themselves but also, in principle, denies the distinction between true and false, between good and evil. He silently moves outward from the thought that no [governing] law exists for the religious and moral life, that religion is nothing but a mood, and that each person may do what he wants [with regard to religion]. In practice, no one holds to this theory. Anyone who finds his salvation in a specific religion opposes all the others—and he does so all the more earnestly in proportion to how firmly he believes. Even they who see nothing more to religion than inner affections stand directly opposed to all who regard ideas as an essential element in religion. Moreover, concerning the nature of religion, it is also foolish to regard Buddhism, Islam, and Christianity—Romanism and Protestantism—as ascending gradations of the same truth. If the pope is the infallible vicar of Christ, then the Reformation was a great error and sin. If the Mass was instituted by Christ, then the Protestant sacrament is judged.

On this basis, no one can one argue that despite the distinction in ideas, the affections of the inner life [*gemoedsaandoeningen*] are nonetheless the same across the different religions. According to precise psychological analysis, this is simply not so. Naturally, there is overlap among the religions on this point. Belonging to one genus, all religions have common characteristics. They all contain dogmatic, cultic, and ethical elements. In all, there is a certain idea of God, sin, redemption, and so forth. But just as the ideas differ from one another and are often diametrically opposed, so the inner affections differ. Indeed, the same powers of the soul are set in motion, but on account of the ideas, those powers are led in different directions and have different persons and occasions as their objects. The love that binds a man to his legal wife is [rooted in] the same power of the soul as that of another person who lives in sin with his concubine. But who would deduce from this that in both cases, the inner affections bear the same character and differ only in inconsequential forms? And yet, this is taught by the romantics and is still proclaimed to ruinous effect in the field of art. But this anarchy in morality does not take a single earnest man into account. It stands in direct conflict with the moral law. And in the same way, indeed, it acts even worse than this when it recognizes no law in the field of religion and takes mood and emotion to be sufficient without burdening itself with the character or direction [of the religion]. Rather, it can be concluded as follows: if God has regulated the conduct of men among themselves in his moral law, then it is obvious that he has much more carefully defined the conduct of men toward him. The commandments of the second table of God's law are constructed upon the first.[8]

We arrive at the same result along a different path, namely, that the different religions cannot be considered mere gradations of the differing revelations of the same God. Christianity claims its own, independent place in the midst of all the religions, even to the point that it judges all of these as false religions, as idolatries. The whole of Scripture is replete with this: that as the Son, the Word, the image of God, Christ has declared God to us and revealed his name to us. The experience of the church corresponds to this. Thousands and millions of Christians have professed, and do confess, that by believing in this gospel they have become partakers of God, whom they knew not before, and have received a life that is diametrically opposed to their own sinful nature. They learned with Paul to boast in peace with God through the blood of the cross. If this experience of believers from every age is true, rather than a fantasy—in other words, if the Christian religion is an independent religion, specifically

8. Here Bavinck refers to the "two tables" of the Ten Commandments, the first four of which refer to human conduct toward God, and the following six, toward other humans. See Ex. 20.—Eds.

distinct from other religions—this can only be explained and is only due to a special revelation that comes to us in Christ. This specific and unique quality and the particularity of the Christian religion stand and fall by the special revelation to which they owe their origin.

At this point, discussion of the question of whether special revelation is supernatural is unnecessary. In a certain sense, all truthful revelation is supernatural with regard to its origin and content, which is to say that, understood properly, all revelation presupposes a world behind and above this one, which enters into this one and makes itself knowable to us by usual or unusual means. All revelation presupposes that as a personal essence, God is distinguished from the world and yet works upon us through and in that world. Naturalism and revelation are irreconcilable. But, be that as it may, the particularity of the Christian religion presupposes the specificity of the revelation that gave it existence. Ultimately, this has always been the doctrinal struggle in the Christian church. In the last instance, it was always about the particularity, the independence, or—if you prefer a less precise but more commonly used term—the absolute character of Christianity. In the struggle against Ebionism[9] and Gnosticism,[10] against

9. Ebionism was an early Jewish sect that taught that Jesus was merely a mortal human being, but was chosen by God to be the Messiah on account of his adherence to the Mosaic law.—Eds.

10. *Gnosticism* is an umbrella term referring to a range of early Jewish and Christian sects that regarded the material world as flawed or evil, and salvation as found in mystical, secret, or esoteric insight.—Eds.

Arianism[11] and Sabellianism,[12] against Pelagianism[13] and Manichaeism,[14] there was always the [same] point of difference: Is Christianity *the* religion, the only, the true religion, or is it only one form of religion among many? Principally and centrally, the question is decided by the place one gives to Christ. What do you think of Christ? That is, that was, and that remains the question of the ages.

Now it is well beyond doubt that the posture of anyone who personally accepts Christ is not ultimately determined through mere intellectual consideration. It is true that the church can produce very sound proofs for its confession of the Christ. Any movement that arises against that confession in the name of Scripture, and then arises against Scripture in the name of Christ, ultimately terminates with the recognition that the church was built on the foundation of the apostles and prophets. But the relationship to Christ that [a believer] enters and, from then on, [follows] toward all the revelation in Scripture is not the fruit of logical reasoning, but, rather, is connected to deep, religious-ethical motives. According to Dr. Bruining,[15] among the modern

11. Arianism was an early Christian heresy that taught that Jesus was the first created thing, through whom all else was created.—Eds.

12. Sabellianism was an early Christian heresy in which the three persons of the Godhead were viewed as three modes of God, rather than three coexistent persons.—Eds.

13. Pelagianism was an early Christian heresy that denied that original sin had corrupted human nature.—Eds.

14. Manichaeism was an ancient religion that held to a dualistic (spirit and matter) cosmology in which the struggle between good and evil is played out in history through the ascetic life and the soul's deliverance from matter.—Eds.

15. Albertus Bruining (1846–1919), a Dutch ethical theologian.—Eds.

theologians there is also a group that argues for a place for Christology in dogmatics on the grounds of the immense significance of the person of Christ not only for the religious development of humanity but also for our personal religious lives.[16]

The experience of the church is similar, but deeper and richer. In its own awareness, its religious and moral life is inseparably connected to the person of Christ. From where, for example, should a man who is guilty before the face of God derive confidence in order to draw near to God, to call God his Father, to put his trust in him for everything in life and death, if God himself had not come to us in Christ [and] reconciled the world to himself, and did not hold our sins against us? If Christ had merely been an ordinary man also, even if he had been a "hero of the religious-moral domain," his message of the forgiveness of sins would be a fallible and untrustworthy human word. And if he only spoke this word without God's purpose for sin having been accomplished in his suffering and death, he did nothing—if understood correctly—but fight against the mistaken notion that God would punish sin and be angry with the sinner. [In that case, it is] not the pious, who stoop under the weight of their guilt, but

16. A. Bruining, "Over de methode van onze dogmatiek," *Teyler's theologisch tijdschrift* 1 (1903): 445. Likewise, if the modern persuasion still believes in the existence of sin, in the essential distinction of good and evil, in the power of the good, in the moral destiny of man, the immortality of the soul, in God as Father in heaven, then it does so not on the basis of intellectual proofs, as the pure application of the empirical method, but, rather, it comes to these [beliefs] along a wholly different path and in fact pays tribute to the religious-ethical method. Allard Pierson, *Gods wondermacht en ons geestelijk leven* (Arnhem: Thieme, 1867), 65.

the godless, who live carelessly toward [God], who are actually proved right by him. The forgiveness of sins then becomes a term that only fits an outdated point of view. And sin is then an act that is considered a punishable offense not by God but only by humans from their legal vantage point. And yet, that is not really sin. And unless something else happens, no one who takes sin seriously and recognizes its unholy character can suddenly just regard himself to be a child of God and count on his grace. The gospel of the forgiveness of sins can fully remove our consciousness of guilt only when, at the same time, it fully proclaims the indissolubility of the moral law. Only then can we believe, [as those] righteous before God, that when our conscience accuses us, God—without any merit on our part—out of sheer grace reckons the righteousness of Christ to us. As such, there is an inseparable connection between the forgiveness of guilt, in which the church glories, and the person and work of Christ. A similar connection can also be pointed to between the revelation that comes to us in Scripture and all the religious and moral experiences of the church concerning the kinship between God and his people, the new birth and the renewal of life, the confidence of faith and the boldness of prayer, endurance and the hope of glory. Revelation and religion are correlates. The latter impoverishes to the same extent that the former is restricted. Whoever denies revelation in nature and history and only allows it to exist as a work of God in the inner life not only takes away the foundation on which religion rests but also gives [religion] up to arbitrariness and bigotry; even idolatry lives on the basis of supposed revelations. And the true religion proves its truth in this: that it rests on a revelation that not only makes known the whole world as a work of God's hands but also proclaims God's forgiving grace in an utterly unique way, in the face of the unimpeachable enforcement of God's moral order.

12

The Blessing of Christianity for Science

A great deal may now be considered to be firmly [established]: that considered according to its own idea and its practice, religion entails belief in its own objective truth and within this, [belief] in the existence and knowability of God, as well as belief in a general and a special revelation. The history of religions puts this beyond all doubt. They who allow the essence of religion to be nothing more than vague moods and indefinite affections have arrived at this [view] not through impartial historical research but through philosophical considerations. But even though representations are an essential element of each religion, they still have this peculiarity: that unlike scientific insights, they are not the fruit of sense perception or intellectual reasoning but always root themselves in the depths of the heart as indubitable faith convictions and cohere with the most intimate life of man. Each religion, even the most degenerate, concerns the highest and holiest [of all] that the human being knows [*kent*]. At the various stages of development, whatever one considers to be the most real, the highest, the true life, that is also the content and subject of religion.[1]

As such, by its very nature, each religious confession lays claim on the entire world. If each religion is accompanied by a certain view of the world and humanity, of nature and history—which it always is—then through this it *binds* the whole of a person's life and also, specifically, [his] science. The degree and extent to which science is bound to these religious convictions can differ, but the principle is always the same. Every religion brings with it a series of ideas that are established for the confessor before, and independently of, all scientific research. In that scientific research, he sets [these religious convictions] down as borders or even lays them as foundations. Every believer—and in the field of religion, everyone is a believer, even if he supposedly believes nothing, as this would also be a matter of faith—must desire that his faith

1. Compare with my *De zekerheid des geloofs*, 2nd ed. (Kampen: Kok, 1903), 14. [English: Herman Bavinck, *The Certainty of Faith*, trans. Harry der Nederlanden (St. Catharines: Paideia, 1980), 12–13.—Eds.]

and his science would be united. After all, there is no double truth. Because the human spirit [*geest*] is one, he must strive for an "unified" [*einheitliche*] world-and-life view, which satisfies both heart and intellect [*verstand*].

A man may reduce religion as much as he wants. However, as long as it rightly bears the name of religion, it is accompanied by a number of ideas that drive scientific research in a certain direction and influence the scientific result. Imagine, for example, with Harnack, that the main content of the gospel is boiled down to the fact that God is our Father, that we are his children, and that we owe this knowledge and experience to the mediation of Jesus, to his word and deed, to his life and death.[2]

2. In *The Certainty of Faith*, 66, I write: "Harnack even asserted that the person of Christ does not belong in the original gospel." The *Kerkelijke Courant* of February 19, 1904, criticized this and claimed that I misquoted Harnack and misunderstood his meaning. Indeed, read the words of Harnack in *What Is Christianity?* [trans. Thomas Bailey Sanders (Philadelphia: Fortress, 1986), 144]: "The gospel, as Jesus proclaimed it, has to do with the Father only and not with the Son." [German: *Das Wesen des Christenthums* (Leipzig: Hinrichs, 1902), 91: "Nicht der Sohn, sondern allein der Vater gehört in das Evangelium, wie es Jesus verkündigt hat, hinein."] But the next clause, "as Jesus proclaimed," does not change the main idea, because according to Harnack, the gospel plays out entirely between God and the soul, and the soul and its God. The tax collector in the temple, the widow with her mite, and the prodigal son knew nothing of a "Christology." Jesus does not assign himself a mediatorial role in the gospel. It is true, Harnack adds, that Jesus in some way knew the Father (without explaining fully how he came to that utterly unique knowledge of God); that through his word and still more by what he did and suffered, he led many to the Father and made the Father known to them; and that which he did by his personal life, through his life crowned with death, shall continue to play a crucial, ongoing role into the future. But taken together, this is nothing other than [the idea] that by his word and example, Jesus continues to produce aftereffects in history, as is the case with all great men in their fields. The *Kerkelijke Courant* itself also says: "The Lord's Prayer says nothing of 'Christology' in the usual sense of the word; [it offers no] peculiar conception of 'the Son' in his essence, origin, [or] dignity, or of a faith in him that must come before faith in the Father. The tax collector in the temple, the woman at the offering box, and the prodigal son had no knowledge of these things, and yet they were justified by Jesus's word." But if this is so, then Jesus's word and life may be the origin and source of the gospel, but his person and work do not matter for its essence and content.

This short confession then entails a whole world-and-life view that binds science from every side. In it, much lies locked up: the existence, the unity, the personality, the fatherhood of God; his creation, maintenance, and governance of the world; the unity of the human race; the special relationship of God to the human being; the leading of God in history, especially in the origin of Christianity; the redemption of humanity through the influence emanating from the person of Jesus; [and] the ultimate triumph of the kingdom of God. With this, all materialistic, pantheistic, and deistic science is negated in advance, without investigation. With "presuppositionlessness" [*Vorauszetzungslosigkeit*], in principle this happens in one fell swoop. This short confession sets us on a theistic basis and means that on a number of cardinal questions

Here the question arises regarding whether Christ belongs *in* the gospel and whether there should then be a specific section on Christ (*locus de Christo*) in the body of dogmatics. Dr. Bruining understood this very well when he said: "There is no place for Christ, the founder of Christianity, in dogmatics which does not deal with history. Christ, the forerunner and leader in the field of the religious life, belongs in the chapter on God's revelations, in the discussion on mediated revelation, and certainly has a prominent place there, but [he is there] among many others as well. Christ, the God-man—and as such, the mediator between God and the world of man, the one through whom God has newly implanted to humanity the knowledge and power for the realization of the ideal—this alone can be the object of a distinct locus of dogmatics." A. Bruining, "Over de methode van onze dogmatiek," *Teyler's theologisch tijdschrift* 1 (1903): 449. Harnack's teaching concerning Jesus recalls Schleiermacher's words: "And He never made His school equivalent to His religion, as if His idea were to be accepted on account of His person, and not His person on account of His idea. Nay, He would even suffer his mediatorship to be undecided, if only the spirit, the principle from which His religion developed in Himself and others were not blasphemed." Friedrich Schleiermacher, *On Religion: Speeches to Its Cultured Despisers*, trans. John Oman (London: Paul, Trench, Trubner, 1893), 172. [German: "Nie hat er seine Schule verwechselt mit seiner Religion, als sollte man um seiner Person willen seine Idee annehmen, sondern nur um dieser willen auch jene; ja, er möchte es dulden, dasz man seine Mittlerwürde dahingestellt sein leisz, wenn nur der Geist, das Princip, woraus sich zijne Religion in ihm und andern entwickelte, nicht gelästert wird." Friedrich Schleiermacher, *Ueber die Religion* (Leipzig: Brockhaus 1868), 229.

in geology, anthropology, psychology, history, the study of Scripture, the person of Christ, and so on, we cannot possibly be neutral, unprejudiced researchers. Among the moderns here in the Netherlands, too, there are those who declare they cannot and may not rest until they have made the philosophical presuppositions and underlying ideas of the Christian religious faith acceptable through the philosophy of our time. If we want to maintain the religious faith in its old, full strength and worth—as we hear them say through Prof. Bruining—then we must force philosophy to incorporate religion into its systems. Then we theologians must arise as leaders in the field of philosophy. Only in this way can we ensure religious faith the recognition and place it deserves and, with this, ensure that religion is kept safe.[3]

From a modern perspective this verdict is meaningful. It implies that religion may indeed make its considerable presence felt on scientific terrain, and that theologians themselves must take the lead in philosophy. If the same were asserted from the orthodox side, it would most likely be taken as an extreme presumption. And yet, although we shall leave this way of putting it for now, in principle there is nothing implicit in it other than that which is involuntarily recognized and confessed by every religious person who believes in truth. Religious faith

3. Albertus Bruining, "The aggressive character of liberal-religious faith," in *Religion and Liberty: Addresses and Papers at the Second International Council of Unitarian and Other Liberal Religious Thinkers and Workers*, ed. P. H. Hugenholtz Jr. (Leiden: Brill 1904), 177–78.

must demand that science take it into account. Which religious faith is the true and perfect one cannot be decided by any earthly tribunal. Ultimately, each [person] must decide this personally, in his conscience, before God. If Roman Catholics submit to the pope, if the Reformed accept Holy Scripture as God's word, if the modern [theologian] conforms to the voice of his conscience, then it rests upon a personal choice for everyone. Of course, this is not to say that how the choice turns out is indifferent as long as it is made sincerely. After all, subjective sincerity is not proof of objective truth. But as humans, we have no right to coerce each other in matters of religion; here each person stands or falls as his own master. Here on earth, error and truth, tares and wheat remain alongside one another in every age. They grow together until the day of harvest. And he who in the end can and will bring about the full, pure separation [between them] is God alone. That is what the Reformers pronounced against Rome in their teaching on the "ability of Holy Scripture to interpret itself" [*facultas Sacrae Scripturae se ipsam interpretandi*]. The truth must achieve her victory not through violence or oppression, not by state power or coercion, but in the royal way of liberty.

Therefore, Christian science also has a right to exist. If each religious persuasion may be applied to the field of science, if each religious confession is of such a nature that it affects and must affect scientific research and results, then in no way may this conviction, which has been known for centuries as the Christian [view], be reduced—in all its justification and freedom—to unscientific dogmatism and done away with. Indeed, nowadays, for many, the idea that Christianity is hostile to all culture, especially to science and art, is dominant. But this view is just as one-sided and exaggerated as the earlier widely held idea that Christianity was nothing other than the gospel of humanity. In this regard, a similarly dominant fashion [can be seen] in clothing and furniture. Because the apostolic witness was made subject to one's own judgment, people have made of Jesus whatever they themselves most preferred. Kant saw in him a divine personification of the sonship of humanity. Renan announced him the adversary of the priesthood. Proudhon[4] turned him into a social reformer. Schopenhauer[5] exalted him to a symbol of the "negation" [*Verneinung*] of life. And others have remolded him as a theosophist, an ascetic, or an ecstatic, or have seen in him the purest type of the Aryan or Germanic race.[6] In fact, people take only a few features from the image of Christ in the New Testament that are comfortable to the present-day way of thinking and try to construct an ideal Christ to suit modern taste. But such a scientific theology can make no claim on truth.[7]

4. Pierre-Joseph Proudhon (1809–1865), a French socialist philosopher and, notably, the first self-described anarchist.—Eds.

5. Arthur Schopenhauer (1788–1860), a German philosopher who rejected idealism in favor of an atheistic, materialistic philosophy.—Eds.

6. Heinrich Weinel, *Jesus im neunzehnten Jahrhundert* (Tübingen: Mohr, 1903).

7. Otto Pfleiderer, *Das Christusbild des urchristlichen Glaubens* (Berlin: Reimer, 1903), 6.

And yet, there is no doubt that Jesus did not emerge as a reformer of state and society, nor did he dedicate his life to the practice of art and science. Rather, he came to bring something entirely different and higher. In his person, his word, and his work, he brought us the gospel of God's grace. He established the kingdom of God on earth and, through his righteousness, has unlocked access [to that kingdom] for us. The gospel is the message of salvation for guilty and lost sinners. This is what it is and must remain. But that is exactly why it is an abundant blessing for the whole person, for the world and humanity, for state and society, for art and science.

The first thing that science owes to this gospel is the reality of an eternal, incorruptible truth. The concept of science did not first arise through Christianity. The whole history of humankind has been a search for truth. Science arose in particular in Greece, and the concept [of science] was imagined by Greek philosophers. But whatever astute investigations were made, and whatever lasting results were obtained, science itself could not remain on the heights reached in the days of Socrates, Plato, and Aristotle. It was later made subservient to practical purposes and came to a halt, like the whole of ancient culture. It did not offer unity; it did not satisfy the heart. The world in all its wisdom did not know God.

Christianity then saved science. The gospel was the proclamation of an eternal, undeniable, indubitable truth, which was revealed in Christ. Through this, the science that had sunk into skepticism was dug out of its decay. "The concept of absolute truth only came into the world (through the monotheistic religions of the Jews, Christians, and Muslims)."[8] The tacit assumption of all science is that there is a sovereign, unchangeable truth, and that it is knowable to the human being. Christianity has now made known such a truth. [In Christianity,] the truth is not a subjective idea, not the mutual relations of human ideas, but, rather, it is an objective reality that stands high above and yet remains accessible to the human being. Through this, science is given a fixed, strong, and essential foundation. For if there is no certainty to be had in matters of religion and morality, and in respect to the unseen, spiritual things, science loses a great deal of its value. It runs the risk also of falling prey of skepticism in other fields and is threatened with decay and ruin as a whole.

It is true that today science enjoys a position of considerable privilege. [In doing so,] it still stands, in part, on Christian foundations. But to the same degree that [science] undermines [Christianity], [science] also works for its own destruction. The evidence for this is already present. While, on the one hand, skepticism, weariness of life, [and] despair of the truth are increasing, people also cast themselves in desperation into the arms of the

8. Emile du Bois-Reymond, cited in Martin von Nathusius, *Das Wesen der Wissenschaft und ihre Anwendung auf die Religion: Empirische Grundlegung für die theologische Methodologie* (Leipzig: Hinrichs, 1885), 117. [German original: "Der Begriff einer absoluten Wahrheit gelangte eigentlich erst durch sie in die Welt."]

grossest superstition. There is also no guarantee that the culture in which we boast will never be taken from us. In spite of their great flourishing, the [cultures] of Babylon and Assyria, of Greece and Rome collapsed. Who shall predict the future of the civilization in which we now participate? And who does not sometimes shudder at the thought of dangers faced in Communism, Africa, and Asia?[9]

> No, the belief in humanity's seamless progress (of the sort imagined by Hegel) should be abandoned. As von Wilamowitz-Moellendorff said in his imperial speech "World Epochs" [*Weltperioden*]: "There is no need to speculate on this. The world teaches by experience that things do not always progress forward, and that the gains made by human labor, which seemed so secure, can be lost. Culture can die, and has done so at least once. The jackal howls in Ephesus, where Heraclitus and Paul preached. Thorns grow rampant in the marble halls of a hundred cities in Asia Minor, where now, only a few stout barbarians cower. Desert sand swirls over the divine garden of Cyrene. Why [recall] these pictures from afar? Anyone who has ever thought about the Roman Forum must have realized that the belief in eternal continuous progress is delusional." Evil is too resistant, too great, and

9. Here Bavinck refers to "red, black, and yellow dangers"—expressions of geopolitical anxiety in that period referring to colonial wars brewing in East Asia and Southern Africa, and to the prospect of a homegrown socialist revolution led by Kuyper's political adversary Pieter Jelles Troelstra (1860–1930).—Eds.

too numerous, to be resolved by a simple schema of thesis, antithesis, and synthesis.[10]

By preaching an objective truth, Christianity simultaneously planted belief in and love for the truth in [many] hearts. Just as the existence of an objective truth is the foundation of all science, so the love of truth is its indispensable, subjective prerequisite. At present, the love of truth is in a poor state among people. It is absolutely not a virtue that is innate in all by nature. In daily life, we continually learn by experience that the truth is sacrificed to self-interest. Those who devote themselves to science are usually no exception to this rule. They are no better and no worse than others who work in trade and industry, in state and society. If the truth and self-interest happen to correspond, it is not difficult to be a friend of the truth. However, in the scientific realm, the truth often happens to be in conflict with our wishes, leanings,

10. W. Fickler, "Unter welchen philosophischen Voraussetzungen hat sich bei Hegel die Wertschätzung des Staates entwickelt und wie ist diese zu beurteilen?," in *Zeitschrift für Philosophie und philosophische Kritik*, vol. 122 (1903), 168. German original: "Nein, der Glaube an eine lückenlose Weiterentwicklung der Menschheit (zooals Hegel ze dacht) ist nicht zu halten. 'Es bedarf gar keiner Spekulation; die Welt hat die Erfahrung gemacht, dass es nicht immer aufwärts geht, dass auch, was als unverlierbarer Gewinn der Menschenarbeit geborgen scheint, verloren gehen kann. Die Kultur kann sterben, denn sie ist mindestens einmal gestorben. Der Schakal heult in Ephesus, wo Heraklit und Paulus gepredigt hatten; in den Marmorhallen von hundert kleinasiatischen Städten wuchern die Dornen und kauern nur vereinzelt verkümmerte Barbaren; Wüstensand wirbelt über dem Göttergarten Kyrenes. Doch wozu die Bilder aus der Ferne?' Die Widerstände des Bösen sind viel zu gross und zu zahlreich, als dass zu ihrer Auflösung das an sich ja ganz durchsichtige Schema von Thesis, Antithesis und Synthesis ausreichte." [Here the source Bavinck cites refers to a lecture by Ulrich von Wilamowitz-Moellendorff (1848–1931), a German classical philologist, delivered on the birthday of Frederick III, emperor of Germany, on January 27, 1897. See Ulrich von Wilamowitz-Moellendorff, *Weltperioden* (Göttingen: Dieterisch'sche Univ.-Buchdruckerei, 1897).]

and insights. How often is there not a contradiction between head and heart, between intellect and will, between reason and desire, between duty and inclination! Sharp self-criticism and stern self-denial are necessary in order to remain faithful to the truth and not deny or falsify it by the craftiness of the heart. There is much truth we do not want because it is in conflict with our lives. Here, too, the saying that whosoever loves his life will lose it is applicable. And that makes us understand the gospel, because it teaches us to know [*kennen*] a truth that can only come into our possession by our self-denial. The gospel of Christ gives science an ethical character and consecrates its practice to a priestly work. According to Bacon's beautiful expression, the kingdom of science is like the kingdom of heaven in that we shall not enter it unless we become like little children.

Second, the entirety of the science that bears the name *theology* is indebted to Christianity. This science does not enjoy the favor of the masses today. It is looked down on from all sides, and its scientific character [is] denied. And theologians have contributed to this in many respects by not defending its name and honor, but as soon as some scholar raises his voice against it in the name of science, they quiver, make concessions, and give up bulwark after bulwark. She who was formerly queen of the sciences has often reduced herself into a beggar for the favor of her sisters. She would let go of the pretense of being theology if only she might remain the science of religion!

But, nevertheless, theology is and remains a glorious science that can only be attributed to Christianity and could not exist without the Christian faith. There is also an element of truth in the pagan religions. God leaves no one without witness, and his eternal power and divinity are understood and seen in [his] creatures. But this knowledge of the truth is so mingled with all kinds of error and lies, we cannot speak of theological science [as arising from it]. As soon as scientific thought awoke in Greece, it took up a position not *in* but *adjacent* and *in opposition to* the religious faith of the people. However, the history of the Christian church offers us an exalted spectacle of a science that was born *of* the faith of the church, which had the knowledge of God for its content and continually unfolded that [content] in ever-increasing richness and depth. If [the church] remains faithful to this, if it perseveres in being what it ought to be, the science of the knowledge of God, which is born of the faith of the church, then it still takes up the first and foremost place among the sciences. It owes this preeminence not to the men who practice [theology], although from the days of the apostles on, it can point to an immense host of great and noble [practitioners][11] who can easily

11. We often hear of the *odium theologicum* [literally, "theological hatred"—a turn of phrase that denotes intense ill feeling that arises in debates on theological topics.—Eds.]. This *odium*, however, may be more widely known [than the same phenomenon among scholars in other disciplines], because theologians often deal with questions that penetrate deeply into life and that also awaken interest outside the circle of their profession. It is equally present among practitioners of other sciences, and no less among artists, merchants, shopkeepers, etc. Read how, for ex-

withstand comparison to the greatest of human spirits. Rather, it owes this primacy to the object with which it is concerned. Theology deals with the loftiest subjects, with the deepest convictions, with the most intimate [parts] of human life. It handles questions that are of the highest importance to every person without exception. Of whatever importance mathematical, physical, philological, [or] historical truths may also be, they do not attain the gravity of [the truths] handled by theology.[12] It is not lust for power among theologians that gives it this pole position. Rather, the central meaning religion and morality have for the whole of human life assures it of the long-

---

ample, Haeckel treats his opponents in Eberhard Dennert, *Die Wahrheit über Ernst Haeckel und seine Welträthsel* (Halle: Müllers Verlagsbuchhandlung, 1903), 62.

12. "The slenderest knowledge that may be obtained of the highest things is more desirable than the most certain knowledge obtained of lesser things." [*Minimum quod potest haberi de cognitione rerum altissimarum, desiderabilius est quam certissima cognitio, quae habitur de minimus rebus.*] Thomas Aquinas, *Summa Theologiae*, trans. the Fathers of the English Dominican Province (London: Burns, Oates, and Washbourne, 1920), I, q. 1, art. 5, ad. 1.

Kant: "Whether the world has a beginning [in time] and any limit to its extension in space; whether there is anywhere, and perhaps in my thinking self, an indivisible and indestructible unity, or nothing but what is divisible and transitory; whether I am free in my actions or, like other beings, am led by the hand of nature and of fate; whether finally there is a supreme cause of the world, or whether the things of nature and their order must as the ultimate object terminate thought—an object that even in our speculations can never be transcended: these are questions for the solution of which the mathematician would gladly exchange the whole of his science. For mathematics can yield no satisfaction in regard to those highest ends that most closely concern humanity." [Bavinck cites Kant from Viktor Cathrein, *Glauben und Wissen: Eine Orientierung in Mehreren Religiösen Grundproblemen der Gegenwart für Alle Gebildeten* (Freiburg: Herder, 1903), 233. For the original source, see Immanuel Kant, *Critique of Pure Reason*, trans. Norman Kemp Smith (London: Palgrave MacMillan, 2007), 423.] Schopenhauer: "You do not cease to boast about the reliability and certainty of mathematics. But, what good does it do me to know ever so certainly and reliably what I have no interest in?" Cited in J. J. van Oosterzee, "De Christelijke theologie, de wetenschap des geloofs," *Voor Kerk en theologie: Mededelingen en bijdragen*, vol. 1 (Utrecht: Kemink, 1872), 101. Gauss: "There are many questions that I would regard as infinitely more important to answer than mathematical ones: questions about ethics, about our relationship to God, and about the future, for example." Cited in Cathrein, *Glauben und Wissen*, 234.

standing honorable name *queen of science*. Even Prof. Bruining, [speaking] at a liberal religious congress,[13] has laid down the demand that theologians would once again set the tone in the field of philosophy. However, theology can satisfy this demand only if it has a truth to proclaim that rests on divine authority and commends itself to the conscience of men. After all, if it rejects God's word, what wisdom shall it then have?

In the third place, Christianity is also a blessing to science in general, for the investigation of nature and history. For Ladenburg, in his famous lecture at the gathering of naturalists and medical doctors in Cassel,[14] it was all too easy when he attributed to the Enlightenment [*Aufklärung*] all the progress of recent years that we owe to the natural sciences. If the argument is made against him that the naturalists are destroying the happiness of humanity and undermining belief in immortality, and put nothing but factories and social misery in its place, then he argues in response that the entire new conception of freedom and human rights, the abolition of slavery and serfdom, all societal improvements and social legislation

13. This refers to an address entitled "Does Religion Presuppose a Theistic Worldview?" ("Godsdienst onderstelt een theistische wereldbeschouwing?"), given by Bruining at a meeting of the Association of Modern Pastors (*Vereniging van modern predikanten*) in 1904. In this address, Bruining argued that religion does not presuppose a prior worldview, and he claimed that religion must be purified of metaphysics. Evidently, Bavinck's use of Bruining's argument that theologians must become active in philosophy and metaphysics is a subversive one. See "Vereen. Van modern predikanten," *Nieuwsblad van het Noorden*, September 14, 1904.—Eds.

14. Albert Ladenburg, *Über den Einfluss der Naturwissenschaften auf die Weltanschauung: Vortrag gehalten auf der 75. Versammlung deutscher naturforscher und Arzte zu Cassel am 21. September 1903* (Leipzig: Verlag von Veit, 1903).—Eds.

are due to the Enlightenment, which was brought about, above all, by the natural sciences. Although modern science has been tremendously significant for modern society, it does not follow that all the benefits of modern civilization should be attributed to the natural sciences. Society is not composed so simply; neither does civilization come about so easily. Very many, and very different, factors are at play in this. Thus, if we speak of Christianity as a blessing for science, this in no way means that science exclusively, or in greatest part, is due to Christianity. Science arises not from re-creation but from creation. And the Christian religion is not in the first place aimed at culture. Earthly prosperity, high civilization, [or] scientific development is not the measure of its truth and worth. What the Christian religion offers us above all else is comfort in order to live and to die blessedly. But in precisely this way, it works on the whole person, in the entirety of his life, in all his thinking and acting. And so Christianity also benefits the practice of science in nature and history.

This is the proof that the Christian religion is the only power that can save us, in the long run, from materialism and pantheism, from scientific and ethical skepticism. For many scholars today, there is only one science, namely, the natural [sort]. Literature, history, law, religion, and ethics, which together form the highest goods of humanity, are no longer taken into account, or are at least regarded as inferior. And the sciences that occupy themselves with these have the right and claim to the name of science only if they adopt the method of the natural sciences or let themselves be incorporated by it. The cynical indifference and gross ignorance that exist in many of these men with regard to all the spiritual goods of humanity have been shown in the works of those who represent all manner of directions stemming from Haeckel's work on the "world riddle." And in his much-discussed speech, Ladenburg has provided new and tangible proof of the same: "The mind only became clear when the holiness of the Bible was doubted and, like all books, it was viewed as the work of man."[15] Although the ancient Greeks made a wondrous beginning with scientific research, [Ladenburg argued,] a deep darkness spread over humanity in the Middle Ages. "Ignorance and superstition became the dominant forces, followed by intolerance, the Inquisition, witch hunts, religious madness,"[16] and so on. But Columbus,[17] Copernicus,[18] Kepler,[19] [and] Newton kindled light in that darkness, natural science awoke, and humanity moved forward in great strides. And then people realized that it was a dream, "a presumptuous and utterly unfounded dream that portrayed the human being in a close relationship to

15. Ladenburg, *Über den Einfluss der Naturwissenschaften auf die Weltanschauung*, 5.—Eds.
16. Ladenburg, *Über den Einfluss der Naturwissenschaften auf die Weltanschauung*, 7.—Eds.
17. Christopher Columbus (1451–1506), the Italian explorer credited with discovering the New World.—Eds.
18. Nicolaus Copernicus (1473–1543), the Renaissance polymath.—Eds.
19. Johannes Kepler (1571–1630), the German polymath.—Eds.

his Creator, who was said to have created him in his own image."[20] That the Bible contains no relevation of supernatural essence that is available to us is clear. "The Old Testament is the work of highly imaginative men, and the New Testament cannot be of divine origin."[21] Miracles have never happened. "Everything that occurs in nature is natural, and the supernatural arises from the brains of dreamers and the ignorant."[22] God cannot be thought of as anything else than a "personification" [*Verkörperung*] of natural laws. And the wish for immortality has been [nothing more than] the father of thought.

In this way, in a short speech of a few pages, the worldview of the whole of humanity was judged. Now, when [Ladenburg's voice] was a lonely one, we could pass by it in silence. But after thousands upon thousands of copies of Haeckel's *The Riddle of the Universe* were sold, despite all the warranted criticism [of it], Prof. Ladenburg delivered this speech at a prestigious meeting of German naturalists and medical doctors, receiving thanks and applause [from them], [and] an overabundance of praise in the newspapers. When we bring this together with many other developments in science, literature, and art, it is clear that in popular culture, notwithstanding the revival of idealism among some men of science, the

20. Ladenburg, *Über den Einfluss der Naturwissenschaften auf die Weltanschauung*, 16.—Eds.

21. Ladenburg, *Über den Einfluss der Naturwissenschaften auf die Weltanschauung*, 17.—Eds.

22. Ladenburg, *Über den Einfluss der Naturwissenschaften auf die Weltanschauung*, 24.—Eds.

materialism of a [figure like] Büchner[23] is not decreasing but, rather, steadily gaining ground. It is not simply a few verses of Scripture but, rather, the whole Christian world-and-life view that Ladenburg fights against—even belief in a personal God and the immortality of the soul. Although he does not go as far as Strauss[24] and expresses himself more modestly, nothing is left untouched. With a view of such developments, concern rather than alienation should be roused, [so that] the Christian side warns against the danger a materialistic direction poses to our whole culture—not only to religion and Christianity, but also to ethics, law, truth, science, and art. And [this warning] has a claim to sympathy and support if here and elsewhere an effort is made to build our culture, and within that, also our science, afresh on Christian foundations, and so to make secure the future. Indeed, we must gratefully acknowledge that a revived philosophical idealism [is now] putting up a strong fight against this theoretical and practical materialism. But if this idealism is not borne up by the religious, by the Christian faith, it almost always capsizes into pantheism and breaks apart what it first tried to build up. Only the Christian religion can and does protect us from both movements, [precisely because it] maintains the independence of the human spirit

23. Ludwig Büchner (1824–1899), a German philosopher and leading advocate for scientific materialism.—Eds.

24. David Friedrich Strauss (1808–1874), a German liberal theologian who argued that modern Europeans should recognize that they are no longer Christians and instead should follow a new, scientifically grounded faith.—Eds.

and grants him an independent place in and toward the world. It reveals a kingdom of unseen and eternal things to us, where the human becomes connected, where he can become a citizen, [a realm] that bears and supports him, and strengthens him against nature, giving an incorruptible meaning to his person, to his vocation and labor. The history of the sciences brings into view how this religious idealism has been beneficial to the practice of science. In part, this already applies to men like Socrates, Plato, and Aristotle, who, to the shame of many Christians, made diligent use of the light given to them. But it is especially true of all those men of science and art in the previous centuries who saw the Christian faith not as an obstacle but as an incentive to their scientific work. It is widely thought [today] that all those men who advanced science [in the past] belonged to the ranks of the "unbelievers." For most of them, though, the opposite is true.[25] And this connection between faith and science would be seen much more clearly in the history of different sciences, especially of philosophy, if it did not systematically conceal the religious principles of the [great] thinkers. More emphasis should fall on this: that in its noblest form, the newer practice of [the study of] nature and history either

25. See Otto Zöckler, *Gottes Zeugen im Reich der Natur* (Gütersloh: Bertelsmann, 1881); Eberhard Dennert, *Die Religion der Naturforscher* (Berlin: Berliner Stadtmission, 1901); K. A. Kneller, *Das Christenthum und die Vertreter der neueren Naturwissenschaft* (Freiburg: Herder, 1903).

Groen van Prinsterer therefore quite rightly considered an appeal to "the alliance of the ancestors" as not inappropriate. Guillaume Groen van Prinsterer, *Ongeloof en Revolutie* (Amsterdam: Höveker, 1868), 17.

consciously or unconsciously presupposes the thoughts of Christianity.[26] Nature and history are implicitly conceived of by their most prominent investigators precisely as Christianity has made them known to us. And conversely, their practice goes in the wrong direction to the same extent that, either intentionally or not, they turn their backs on the Christian worldview. For example, for many years, materialistic natural science has fixed our attention on the mechanism of nature, on the randomness and purposelessness of all its phenomena, on the activity of all nature's power as unconcerned with moral law.[27] To a certain degree, they were right in doing so, in view of the fantastical deification of nature that had become dominant under the influence of idealism. But it has just as one-sidedly passed over into another extreme. It has "de-divinized" [*entgöttert*] nature. And now, to many, that same nature, especially since its mysteries have become known, has become an incomprehensible, horrifying, demonic power. So it is often portrayed in literature and art. Indeed, it is viewed as such because of ever-increasing superstition. God has disappeared from [nature], and the devil has taken his place. For Nietzsche, the entire concept of nature is gone. For him, the world is chaos, without order, without law, without thought.

26. See Herman Bavinck, *Reformed Dogmatics*, ed. John Bolt, trans. John Vriend, vol. 3, *Sin and Salvation in Christ* (Grand Rapids, MI: Baker Academic, 2006), 38. [Dutch original: Herman Bavinck, *Gereformeerde Dogmatiek*, vol. 3 (Kampen: Bos, 1898), 23.]

27. Cf. Ernst Haeckel, *Die Welträthsel: Gemeinverständliche Studien über Monistische Philosophie* (Bonn: Stauss, 1899), 295.

On the question posed by him "When will we complete our de-deification of nature?"[28] there is but one answer: when all rule, all order, all measure, all logos is gone from nature and therefore nature itself is gotten rid of. The same thing will happen to history without the Christian faith. If there is no personal God who rules all things by his providence, upon which ground will we still believe that there is meaning, a plan, a progression in history? Schopenhauer perceived this. He denied any progress in the historical process. History is for him only an eternal, meaningless repetition of the misery into which the blind will to live [*levenswil*] throws itself. While Hegel described all reality as reasonable, Schopenhauer saw nothing in it but unreasonableness. And indeed, if, according to historical materialism, thinking is not the origin of being but, rather, being is the origin of thinking, then in principle the presupposition of all science—that hiding in all things are thought and idea, measure and number—falls away. This [presupposition] can only be maintained from the standpoint of Christian theism, which shows us a work of God in nature, and in history makes us recognize the leading of his almighty hand.

Within this great, all-controlling agreement between the Christian religion and the presuppositions [that undergird] science, the differences that exist between the

28. Here Bavinck cites Friedrich Nietzsche, *Die fröhliche Wissenschaft* (Chemnitz: Verlag von Ernst Schmeitzner, 1882), 139. German original: "Wann werden wir die Natur ganz entgöttlicht haben?" English translation: *The Gay Science*, trans. Walter Kaufmann (New York: Vintage, 1974), 169.—Eds.

two are of relatively little importance. In and of themselves, they are undoubtedly of great importance, as they concern the origin of the world and humankind, the revelation of God in Israel and in the person of Christ. But in *principle* all these differences are determined by Christian theism. They are all focused on the question of miracles. If the answer were only as easy as Prof. Ladenburg's, who simply decrees that "everything that occurs in nature is natural, and the supernatural arises from the brains of dreamers and the ignorant,"[29] then it would not be worth the effort to waste another word on it. But miracle [*wonder*] stands in the closest connection to the confession of theism and is of the deepest religious-ethical significance. Miracle is the proof that the mechanism is subordinate and subservient to teleology, natural order [*physis*] to *ethos*, the world to the kingdom of God, and nature to grace. If there is no supernatural, if God is not to be thought of other than as the "personification" [*Verkörperung*] of natural laws, if there is no higher power than that which works in nature, then the human spirit is subjugated to matter, the religious-ethical life loses its foundation, and belief in the triumph of the good is a vain dream. This is why Titius rightly called belief in miracle [*wondergeloof*] the energy and apex of faith in God's providence.[30] Its conflict with the order of nature is so

29. Ladenburg, *Über den Einfluss der Naturwissenschaften auf die Weltanschauung*, 24.—Eds.

30. Arthur Titius, *Religion und Naturwissenschaft: Eine Antwort an Professor Ladenburg* (Tübingen: Mohr, 1904), 92.

minimal that [nature] rightly presupposes and confirms it. Furthermore, it is in no way in conflict with the facts and methods of natural and historical science, because it leaves them fully intact and is itself, by virtue of its nature, withdrawn from the judgment of these sciences. Just as physiological psychology can follow the stimulations of nerves from our senses into the brain but then suddenly finds itself before the mystery of [our] perceptions, so can natural and historical science approach the border of the miraculous but cannot pass beyond it. There a mysterious power then appears, which they acknowledge in faith but, by the nature of the matter, can never understand or explain.

For all these reasons a connection and cooperation of Christian confession and scientific research is not only possible but also useful and necessary. Religion and science *cannot* fight each other. Motivated by fear, their divorce might seem like the surest way to keep religion safe for a while. In the long run, though, this will not satisfy anyone. It is untenable both in practice and in theory. How could it ever be defensible to suppose that a man, because of and in proportion to his fear of God, is incapable of the pursuit of science? Rather, godliness is profitable for all things, having the promise for both this life and the life to come. Pious people certainly also have their flaws and one-sidedness. But this takes nothing away from the principle. Love of God cannot be in friction with love of neighbor, nor with the love of science.

To the contrary, it is its foundation, principle, and driving force. The ideal for the scientific researcher cannot be that in his work, his heart's deepest and noblest convictions are kept silent. Rather, it is much more that he is a man of God who is perfectly equipped for every good work. [As identities,] human being and child of God, human being and Christian, cannot be in conflict. The best Christian is also the best human.

13

A Christian University

Ultimately, these principles regarding the relationship between Christianity and science call for embodiment in a Christian university. This idea is not new. Until the beginning of the previous century, all schools—not only of lower but also of higher education—took a decidedly Christian, even confessional-ecclesiastical position. On the other hand, what is new is what Prime Minister Kuyper has called the "indifferent" system, the purportedly neutral view of the concept of science. And while the old system had earned its admirers, the new view must prove not only its validity but also its possibility and durability.

What has been seen of it thus far has not shown its [claim to] impartiality in a flattering light. Neutrality existed primarily as an accommodating attitude toward all negative trends but turned into excessive partiality as soon as it was confronted by those who profess a positive Christian faith. The persecution of the Seceders [*Afgescheidenen*][1] serves as striking proof of this. When Da Costa[2] dared to express objections to the spirit of the age, he was shunned like a leper in Amsterdam. When Van Oosterzee issued a mild critique of Scholten's *Doctrine of the Reformed Church*,[3] the general fairness of which is recognized by all, the death knell sounded for his scientific reputation in Leiden. And these cases are not alone. They could easily be multiplied from the lives of Chantepie de la Saussaye[4] and Beets,[5] from Groen van Prinsterer and Kuyper. In recent years, a change for the better has been apparent. Liberalism's awkward teenage years [*vlegeljaren*] are over. The hubris of science is broken. The government's proposal for special professorial

1. Bavinck is referring to members of the Christian Reformed Church, which broke away from the Dutch Reformed Church in the Secession (*Afscheiding*) of 1834. Prior to the introduction of full religious freedom in the new liberal constitution in 1848, membership of the Christian Reformed Church was illegal and entailed sustained state-led persecution. See James Eglinton, *Bavinck: A Critical Biography* (Grand Rapids, MI: Baker Academic, 2020), 3–40.—Eds.

2. Isaäc da Costa (1798–1860), a Dutch Sephardic Jew, converted to Christianity and played a prominent role in the Dutch *Réveil*—a revival movement among Dutch Reformed Christians that emphasized personal experiential piety.—Eds.

3. Jan Hendrik Scholten, *De leer der Hervormde Kerk in hare grondbeginselen*, 2 vols. (Leiden: Brill, 1848–1850). An avowedly heterodox theologian, Scholten (1811–1885) was Bavinck's *Doktorvater* at Leiden University.—Eds.

4. Daniel Chantepie de la Saussaye (1818–1874), a theologian at the University of Groningen.—Eds.

5. Nicolaas Beets (1814–1903), a Dutch theologian.—Eds.

chairs [*bijzondere leerstoelen*] was favorably received, and the claim that science on the basis of belief in revelation is impossible is now proclaimed with less gusto than it used to be. But [the historical novelty of] this change is greatly overestimated by Prof. Van der Vlugt,[6] who views the proposed legislation regarding special universities [*bijzondere universiteiten*] as an anachronism.[7] After all, that change is not a fruit of the liberal principle but a consequence that is due, rather, to the restless struggle against it by the Christian side. By nature, it is accidental rather than principial. It arose from a change of circumstances, not from conviction. Mr. Troelstra[8] not only stated blatantly that dogma and science are incompatible but also declared that the Social Democrats are very pleased with the situation that exists at the public universities[9] and would want to bring about no change to this.[10] The struggle for the character of science and the university is far too deep to be resolved by a few well-intentioned statements. The struggle touches upon the deepest religious-ethical principles. As the secretary of state[11] compellingly argued in his speech in the Second Chamber,[12] it is a struggle between the Christian and that which is not positively Christian,

6. Willem van der Vlugt (1853–1928), a Dutch jurist, professor, and liberal politician.—Eds.

7. *Handelingen van de Tweede Kamer* (1904), 1278.

8. See chap. 12, n. 9 (p. 188).—Eds.

9. The situation in question was that public schools and state universities received full state funding, whereas religious schools and universities did not.—Eds.

10. *Handelingen van de Tweede Kamer* (1904), 1298–99.

11. As prime minister, Abraham Kuyper was also secretary of state (*Minister van Binnenlandse Zaken*).—Eds.

12. *Handelingen van de Tweede Kamer* (1904), 1306, 1436.

between the old and new world-and-life views, between creation and development, revelation and evolution. It concerns the recognition, or not, of the facts of sin and redemption, and is dominated by the question What do you think of Christ? And for this reason, when this principial question must be considered, the parties regroup to the right and left, not because of the goodwill of some of the members but because of the logic of principles.[13] It never seems in conflict with the neutrality and unbiased nature of science to proceed from the philosophical principles of Spinoza, Kant, Hegel, Marx, Comte, Scholten, or Opzoomer,[14] but this does seem to be the case when these are placed on the foundation of the confession of Christ according to Scripture.

But regardless of this, the neutral concept and practice of science also clashes with the reality of life. Universities are not castles built in the sky but are rather institutions with a prior history that are bound to all manner of traditions, that stand under the influence of the entirety of their surroundings, and that, to the extent that they have become organs of the state, have lost their freedom and independence. For this reason, Kant was even of the opinion that science was purely represented in the university only by the faculty of philosophy. They alone were free, unprejudiced, and independent, because philosophy was

13. Abraham Kuyper, "Rationalisme," *De Standaard*, March 25, 1904.

14. Cornelis Willem Opzoomer (1821–1892), a Dutch jurist, philosopher, and theologian.—Eds.

exclusively subject to reason and had nothing to serve but the truth. The other faculties, however—theology, law, and medicine—were bound by the laws of the state, church, and society, and had to reckon with the demands of practice and life.[15] Although theoretically an advocate of educational freedom, he [Kant] subordinated it to the advancement of the greatest good for humanity, to the ethical society, and always urged great caution in its practical application. As he said, one must be aware that even if all that one says may be true, one is still not obliged to speak all truth openly. One must carefully set to work on the religion of the people. The Bible and the prevailing religious ideas of the time must be used to further moral conviction and moral community. To bring up objections to the Bible in schools, churches, and popular publications is unwise. Such would only cause people to lose their faith and to give themselves over to complete unbelief. One must be much more aware of the predilection of the people for their old churchly faith and thus introduce the new rational faith gradually. It is advisable for everyone to speak carefully so as not to incur the scandal of having to retract [what one has said] later on. And Kant behaved accordingly. When he published *Religion within the Boundaries of Mere Reason*[16] in 1793 and, as a

15. Immanuel Kant, "The Conflict of the Faculties," in *Religion and Rational Theology*, trans. and ed. Allen Wood and George di Giovanni (Cambridge: Cambridge University Press, 1996), 250.

16. Immanuel Kant, *Religion within the Boundaries of Mere Reason*, trans. and ed. Allen Wood and George di Giovanni (Cambridge: Cambridge University Press, 1998).

result, received a disapproving letter from King Friedrich Wilhelm,[17] he declared that, as a faithful subject of his royal majesty, he would abstain from all open discussion of natural and revealed religion.[18]

The system of absolute educational freedom, in principle, is not defended by anyone and nowhere maintained in practice. But educational freedom must be carefully distinguished from freedom of conscience, of faith, and of the press. In a narrower sense, educational freedom is to understand the right of teachers in educational institutions to speak their views openly and to teach students. In reality, this is limited everywhere and can be nothing else than limited. State interest, public order, old traditions, and good morals allow this freedom to exist, in weaker or stronger degrees, in different places. When a teacher at a state school promulgates nihilism, anarchism, the right of revolution and regicide, suicide, perjury, usury, theft, [and] polygamy, it would not be small-minded to ask whether the state should look upon all this passively. Certainly there is a difference between defending [an idea] with words and the exhortation to [commit] the deed [associated with it], but when students deduce the consequence from the words of their teachers and turn word into deed, there is in abundant reason for the complaint that chopping off branches is

17. Frederick William II of Prussia (1744–1797).—Eds.

18. Ernst Katzer, *Das Problem der Lehrfreiheit und seine Lösung nach Kant* (Tübingen: Mohr, 1903).

not beneficial as long as the axe is not also laid at the root of the tree.

Still, everyone will understand the difficulty faced by the state in stepping forth and acting. First, in the present day, the state is neutral. It no longer has a confession and thus, also, no longer has a standard of judgment. It can only stick to the vague definition of public order and good manners. But, on the other hand, as in all of life and especially in the field of science, it is extremely difficult to hold authority and freedom, preservation and progress in perfect balance. Alongside authority, freedom also has its rights. The new [thing] that is proclaimed arouses mild admiration and opposition but can still later prove to be the truth. However, precisely because the present state lacks the competency and skill [needed] to be attentive to principles and allows, and must allow, all manner of teachings in its [public] universities, it has all the more reason to rejoice over the fact that the people themselves desire and are establishing schools at every level of the educational system that are built on Christian foundations. The private [i.e., Christian] primary schools have been a blessing to our nation, as all will now acknowledge; the state should be neither ashamed nor remorseful that it has gradually adopted a friendlier posture toward them. This is even more the case with the Christian schools for secondary and higher education. Now that the government has lost the opportunity to advance the kingdom of Jesus Christ directly, its moral duty is all the more to support and encourage every effort that the nation itself is employing to that end.

The equity and utility of this is all the more noticeable when one imagines that the universities are not only institutions of science but also institutions of education, schools of training and nurture. The university has a twofold task: the application of science, and training for [the use of academic disciplines] in practice. Even the most idealistic movement must take the university's dual calling into account. A school that existed only for the practice of science would not need or receive students. Those who follow the path of studies do so first and foremost in order to be able to take up a job in church, state, or society. In this respect, too, life precedes philosophy. The motto of practicing science for the sake of science sounds beautiful but finds no support in reality. Through the university, all students seek to earn a living and position in life. But even if this practical goal is of such great importance to the university, it is still not the only goal—certainly not so, in any case, in the German-style universities.[19]

It goes without saying that science, and the practice thereof, is not limited to the walls of a particular school or university, or even to all the universities together, any

19. Friedrich Paulsen, *Die deutschen Universitäten und das Universitätsunterricht* (Berlin: Verlag von A. Asher, 1902). [Here Bavinck's mention of "German-style universities" (*universiteiten van het Duitsche type*) refers to the Humboldtian model of higher education that developed in nineteenth-century Prussia, which emphasized the education of the growing middle class and was directly influenced by Friedrich Schleiermacher.—Eds.]

more than it is bound to any office or occupation, any position or class created by men. It arises freely from the human mind [*geest*], to which God gifted the disposition and desire for any field of knowledge and thought. Across the ages, many have practiced and advanced science who were not educated by or attached to a university. Thus, regardless of whatever nation or era in which they arose, all those who have pointed ignorant and errant humanity in the right direction in any field of knowledge, and who have understood something of God's thoughts in nature or history, belong to the *universitas scientiarum*. But that does not change the fact that by bringing together a group of scientific men, by providing them with a carefree position and putting a treasure chest of valuable resources at their service, the universities gradually became institutions for science. And this practice of science does not stand in enmity against the aforementioned goal, the training of young men for positions in life—although it is often not altogether easy to unite it [to that goal]. This is so because the training for those positions happens at the university and should appropriately happen through *scientific* formation, through the development of independent perceiving and thinking. Indeed, scientific research is the university's foremost means of cultivating men of clear insight and independent judgment.

At present, though, [we often hear] the opinion that such a scientific formation into independent men is possible only when students have the opportunity to listen to professors of different and very divergent outlooks. Judging by this opinion, one would expect that every faculty and each university here and abroad would demonstrate a smorgasbord of professorial principles and systems. The reality, however, looks completely different. In the same faculty, and often across the same university, men of the same persuasion are appointed one after the other; once in a while, as an exception, a professor of different conviction is appointed. And this also lies in the nature of the matter. Professors have the right of nomination[20] and, in the first place, look among their kindred spirits for colleagues with whom they can interact scientifically and amicably. A few years ago, Prof. Van Geer[21] raised a complaint about the manner in which the nomination of professors took place at our public universities, namely, that consulting the faculty for nominations had the downside that all diversity was ruled out, all clashes were avoided, and only friends were nominated.[22] The difference between doctrine and life is great indeed. According to the doctrine, there is room for all, but according to life, only for us and our friends.

[Alongside this,] the aforementioned view is also psychologically and pedagogically untenable. It rests on the erroneous assumption that young people who have just

20. This refers to the right of professors (*het recht van voordracht*) to nominate others for professorial positions, subject to government approval.—Eds.

21. Pieter van Geer (1841–1919), professor of mathematics and physics at Leiden University.—Eds.

22. Pieter van Geer, "Ons Hooger Onderwijs II. De universiteit," *Vragen des tijds* (April 1887): 96–130.

come from gymnasium[23] or higher burger school[24] should already have the desire and aptitude to see for themselves and to make independent choices between different ideas and theories, principles and systems. It secretly includes the idea that the intellect is the highest and almost only thing in man, that everything must be judged by the measure of that intellect, and that authority and faith, heart, and conscience lay hardly any weight in the scale. To our universities, these things are barely taken into account; it is almost as though a man should be embarrassed of them. Professors rarely involve themselves in religious and moral questions; and if they do, they treat them too much as [merely] intellectual concepts, not as realities of life. Even in primary schools, [we] sometimes hear the view being put forth that the teachers themselves have no concern for the behavior of the students outside of the school. School and life [now] stand next to each other. And in the university, the task of education now falls upon the students themselves. They themselves must know [*weten*] what they will become. It is no wonder, then, that now and again, even from within their own camp, a voice rises up warning against this system of education, or rather against this lack of all education in the public universities.[25] How could it also work well pedagogically where young men of about twenty years

23. "Gymnasium," a classical high school.—Eds.

24. "Higher burger school," a type of secondary school developed in the nineteenth century with the aim of preparing pupils for careers in trade and industry.—Eds.

25. Robert Tutein Nolthenius, "Student-zijn," *De Gids* (October 1903): 60–89.

old, whose atypical social circles are almost completely outside ordinary life, and who thus consider all things from a very one-sided viewpoint, conclude that they need not worry about authority and tradition but have to form a world-and-life view by themselves? As Prof. Woltjer[26] remarked last year in the First Chamber, the result of this system can only be that one group of students comes along who are inwardly [i.e., in principle] opposed to the education provided by the professor, are wary of him, and, [because of their] great prejudice [against his principles], reject all that he says. In that scenario, education is as good as fruitless. Meanwhile, another group goes along with the professor and takes what the professor says, on the basis of his authority, as what always happens. And a third group becomes despondent and skeptical, gives up on caring about the principles, and throws themselves into the practical.[27]

Without a doubt, university education requires that students become acquainted with other systems and insights in an evenhanded way. But this can happen just as well in schools that work from decidedly Christian principles as in others that take the so-called neutral standpoint. Although the public universities are also neutral

26. Jan Woltjer (1849–1917), professor of classical languages and literature at the Free University of Amsterdam.—Eds.

27. "Rede van Prof. Woltjer," *De Standard*, February 9, 1903. [Bavinck's text provides the wrong date for this article, February 19. In Woltjer's original address, the second group of students is further described as those who have to take courses under professors whose principles they oppose; the students take such courses in a perfunctory way, aiming to pass, but without being influenced by the professors.—Eds.]

in the sense that, in the abstract, no one is excluded from being a professor or student [simply because] of his confession, the professors and students are not made neutral in the process. Rather, they are usually already committed to a certain world-and-life view that they love and defend, and that guides their research. It would not even be too bold to argue that at present, in general, differing viewpoints are studied more seriously at the Christian universities than at those universities that proceed entirely from the modern worldview and see themselves as in step with the spirit of the age. It is precisely because they take up a [specific] position in the field of science with their Christian confession that they are always compelled to stay meticulously up-to-date with all that is happening in the field of science. The [scientific] works produced by those on the believing side provide abundant witness to this.

Naturally, the objective exposition of another opinion by the professors at a Christian university is then followed by a critique based on the truth of his own world-and-life view, but a professor from a neutral university cannot, and indeed does not, do otherwise [i.e., entertain views other than his own]. If he is not satisfied with [the motto] "I do not teach, I tell" [*je n'enseigne pas, je raconte*],[28] he shall subject the feelings of others to a judgment that, however businesslike and nonpartisan, lays down his own convictions and opinions as a yardstick. Anyone who lives

28. Here Bavinck cites Michel de Montaigne, originally *Je n'enseigne poinct, je ractone.* Michel de Montaigne, *Les essais* (Paris: Abel l'Angelier, 1585), 806.—Eds.

and works from an earnest principle is a propagandist. Even a skeptic is a propagandist for the dogma of doubt. But this method, followed by every professor, does not in the least prevent the students from being impartially informed about the state of scientific research in any given subject, or from being stimulated to independent study.

In practice, then, no one actually follows the prescriptions of the neutral system. Just as the universities and faculties are usually populated—despite their theory—with like-minded men, so do parents send their sons, as a rule, to universities whose principles and directions conform to their own convictions. The difference exists only in that moderns and liberals, radicals and socialists are quite satisfied with the current status quo and receive from the state precisely [the funded] schools that they want for their sons, while those who positively confess to be Christians are not satisfied, and cannot be, precisely because the public universities satisfy the aforementioned groups so resoundingly, whereas [Christians] currently have to provide for themselves what the government denies them. It goes without saying that if all the public schools in the Netherlands were intentionally Roman Catholic or Reformed, all of the aforementioned groups would present their complaint to the government and insist on freedom and equality of rights, just as their opponents are now doing.

A Christian university also enjoys this important advantage over a neutral university: it restores the connection [of science] to life. The condition we are in is *un*healthy. It cannot be good that school and life, science and practice, theology and church are so far from each other, which is the case at the moment. This is most apparent in religion, but it is not only ministers who were trained at the universities and who then honestly and openly proclaim to their congregations what they have heard and learned at the university; it is also lawyers, doctors, teachers, among others, whose religious and moral convictions now usually stand against those of the people. This cannot be the real, normal state of things. If we cannot arrive at a reconciliation between the two, we then run the risk that this dualism will cause the development both of the civilization and of the religion of the people to fall apart—as once happened in the ancient world. In fact, everyone is convinced of this. There are not [separate] esoteric and exoteric sciences;[29] [there is] no double truth.

Thus, one side argues that this conflict can be resolved only if the people radically reimagine their religious and moral concepts and accept the standpoint of contemporary science. In particular, this requirement is always imposed on the church by theology,[30] but in principle we hear this same desire expressed everywhere.

29. Here Bavinck alludes to the Aristotelian distinction between esoteric knowledge (directed only at educated insiders) and exoteric knowledge (directed only at uneducated outsiders).—Eds.

30. Friedrich Delitzsch, *Babel und Bibel: Ein Rückblick und Ausblick* (Stuttgart: Deutsche Verlags-Anstalt, 1904), 9.

The proponents of the modern worldview, evolutionists, moralists, criminologists, among others, exert themselves like this, urging the government to free the people from their old traditions and familiarize them with the pronouncements of modern science from primary school onward. That is why such a fierce war is waged over schooling at every level. It is concerned with the question of whether the Christian worldview or the modern worldview will capture the people and the future. Quite rightly, Dr. Eduard David,[31] the able spokesman of the evolutionistic group of Social Democrats, said that the time for the conquest for political power through revolution had not yet come.

> It is not the gentlemen of the government or the leading men of the opposing parties who withhold political power from us today. No, it is the *popular majority*, standing behind these gentleman, who oppose us, who have not yet entrusted us with the power that we need in order to shape things according to our will. In truth, this idea is not new. But it seems as though our radicals—in their deep speculations—no longer see such simple things. Therefore it should be emphasized again: the as yet unenlightened popular majority is protected by its own reaction; the people are still their own worst enemy; the ignorance of the masses is the only serious obstacle

31. Eduard David (1863–1930), the German Social Democratic politician.—Eds.

> in the way of seizing political power. Once this bulwark has been crossed—who will be able to resist us?[32]

Such words were not preached to deaf ears. However, we have a hope that this bulwark, erected as it was according to the Christian confession of the people, shall withstand this formidable attack. Those who attack it have no comprehension of what would fall if this bulwark were demolished. For whoever takes faith from the people either gives them over to complete unbelief or casts them into the arms of the grossest superstition. Kant feared this danger, and Hegel tried to use the form of illustration to preserve for the people what the philosopher possessed in the form of the concept. And yet, if in principle and essence the religion of the Christian nations is [apparently] the same as the idolatries of the pagan nations, we—like the Greek philosophers—should spare no effort in taking up the fight [against this claim], because error and lies can provide nothing else than the pretense of liberty and false comfort.

---

32. Eduard David, "Die Eroberung der politischen Macht," *Sozialistische Monatshefte* (1904), 204. [German original: "Nicht die Herren von der Regierung, nicht die führenden Geister der gegnerischen Parteien sind es, die ons heute die politische Macht vorenthalten. Nein, die *Mehrheit des Volkes*, die hinter diesen Herren steht, ist es, die uns widerstrebt, die uns die Macht noch nicht anvertraut, deren wir bedürfen, um die Dinge nach unserem Willen zu gestalten. Der Gedanke ist wahrhaftig nicht neu. Aber es scheint, als ob unsere Radicalen bei ihren tiefsinnigen Speculationen so einfache Dinge nicht mehr sehen. Darum sei es hier nochmals scharf betont: *Die Schutztruppe der Reaction ist die noch rückständige Mehrheit des Volkes*; das Volk ist immer noch des Volkes schlimmster Feind; der Unverstand der Massen ist das einzig ernsthafte Hindernis auf der Bahn zur Ergreifung der politischen Macht. Ist erst dies Bollwerk überstiegen—wer will uns dann noch widerstehn?"]

Before we decide to do so and, in fact, despair at [the idea of] reconciliation, we must earnestly consider the question of whether, as regards its principle and method, and also many of its self-styled results, modern science is not on the wrong track. And that question becomes all the more pressing as we consider all that is being presented to the [ordinary] person in the name of science. Who would wish that the theories which have been proclaimed in modern times about the existence of God; about Christ; on the apostles and prophets; on the soul and its immortality; on the origins of humanity and society; on law and morals, sin and crime; on retribution and punishment; on marriage, family, property, [and] murder would be taken up in the popular consciousness and made the compass for life? Not only religion and morality but also society and state would be given over to destruction. As it is interpreted by many of its practitioners today, science is not only set in tension against the confession of the church. It is also set in conflict with the existence and life of humanity. It does not fit with reality. Rather, it subverts it. It destroys rather than explains life. If the politician imagines no higher authority than the will of the people; if the sociologist takes into account nothing but an unconscious impulse and human arbitrariness [when considering] the origin and development of society; if the jurist no longer possesses any eternal norm for law but merely sees it as the fallout of ever-changing relationships; if the criminologist regards the criminal as unlucky or insane and turns the prison into an educational institution; if the moralist erases the distinction between good and evil, and glorifies free love and suicide; if the historian regards history as only the outworking of economic factors; if the psychologist denies the independence of the human soul; if the medical doctor understands nothing more than a gradual difference between his science and veterinary science; if the theologian no longer believes that there is any truth in religion—and so on—it is evident that the very foundations upon which our civilization has rested thus far have been corroded. For this reason, it is not narrow-mindedness but rather a high and holy concern that should drive those who call upon such interpreters of science to enter serious and careful self-reflection before setting themselves up as the reformers of current-day society.

One such voice calls out from the idealism that has recently been revived. But alongside it, there are also those who in principle expect no recovery in science, just as in state and society, other than through a return to the gospel of Christ. A university that places itself on the foundation of this gospel and joins the confession of the church comes into conflict not with science *itself* but only with some, perhaps many, of its current practitioners. And it lays that gospel at the foundation not to bind science but to protect its practitioners—who are always limited, short-sighted, and sinful people, with darkened intellects [*verstand*] and deceptive hearts—from all kinds of error and lies, and to put them in a better position from which to seek and find the truth. Science is always the practice of truth. When one hears some of its advocates speak, it seems as if it is not truth but freedom that is the goal. But this is not so. Freedom is only a means to arrive at the goal, namely, the truth.[33] Freedom is a difficult concept to define in the abstract. Just as it is threatened by servile bondage, on the one side, so on the other it must be on its guard against caprice and debauchery. For science, freedom exists, in the first place, in that it has the right to seek the truth, and when it has found it, to express and defend it. But while on earth there is no infallible institution that can determine what truth is in science, the freedom of science is then, in the second place, in that the different persuasions which actually exist not be hindered by the state or by the church from seeking the truth in the only way in which each, according to its convictions, can find it.

Now, Christians can have no other conviction than this: that on scientific terrain, the truth is found only when one proceeds from the confession that Christ is the way, the truth, and the life, and that no one can come to the Father—also as the origin and ultimate goal of all things—except through him. This confession is not opposed to science, for creation and re-creation have the

33. See Victor Cathrein, *Glauben und Wissen: Eine Orientierung in den religiösen Grundproblemen der Gegenwart für alle Gebildeten* (Freiburg: Herder, 1903), 167.

same origin. Grace does not negate nature but liberates and restores it. Christ came not to destroy the works of the Father but only to destroy the works of the devil. Christ's own confession comes to the aid of science, freeing it from lies and leading scientific research on the right path. To be precise, the name *Christian science* is an abbreviated expression. While it emerges from creation, science itself is neither Christian or unchristian. Science has its standard in the truth. What is true is scientific, even if all the world claims otherwise. And what is untrue is not scientific, even if all people insist that it is. But because there is so much pretense and forgery in science, as there is everywhere, God gave us a guide and a signpost in his revelation, which directs our steps in the practice of science and keeps us from going astray. Thus, Christian science is a science that investigates all things by the light of that revelation and, therefore, sees them as they truly are in their essence. In the eyes of the world this might be foolishness, but the folly of God is wiser than men, just as the weakness of God is stronger than men. "For we cannot do anything against the truth, but only for the truth" [2 Cor. 13:8].

Index